Supporting Pupils with Autistic Spectrum Disorders

Supporting Pupils with Autistic Spectrum Disorders

A Guide for School Support Staff

Lynn Plimley
Maggie Bowen

P·C·P

Paul Chapman
Publishing

Paul Chapman Publishing
A SAGE Publications Company
1 Oliver's Yard
55 City Road
London EC1Y 1SP

SAGE Publications Inc
2455 Teller Road
Thousand Oaks, California 91320

SAGE Publications India Pvt Ltd
B-42, Panchsheel Enclave
Post Box 4109
New Delhi 110 017

Library of Congress Control Number 2006920091

A catalogue record for this book is available from the
British Library

ISBN-10 1-4129-2316-6   ISBN-13 978-1-4129-2316-3
ISBN-10 1-4129-2317-4   ISBN-13 978-1-4129-2317-0 (pbk)

Typeset by C&M Digitals (P) Ltd, Chennai, India
Printed in Great Britain by the Cromwell Press, Trowbridge, Wiltshire
Printed on paper from sustainable resources

Contents

Lynn Plimley

Lynn Plimley originally trained to teach children with Special Educational Needs in the mid-70s, and since 1979 has worked with children with autistic spectrum disorders (ASD). She has worked in generic special schools for primary aged children, residential schools for those with SLD and has been part of a multi-disciplinary team supporting inclusion. She was the first Principal of Coddington Court School in Herefordshire, a provision for children aged 8–19 with ASD.

She works part-time as a Lecturer in ASD at the University of Birmingham on their web-based course (www.webautism.bham.ac.uk). She also tutors M.Ed dissertation students for the Course in ASD (Distance Learning), and is a member of the internationally respected Autism team, based at the University of Birmingham's School of Education, led by Professor Rita Jordan.

Lynn also works for Autism Cymru, establishing a mechanism for mainstream Secondary, Primary and Special school teachers, to share good practice. She offers consultancy as a trainer for any kind of provision for people with ASD, and has built up a national profile of training in the importance of understanding the condition of autistic spectrum disorders for schools and care establishments. Lynn is the Book Editor, and an Editorial Board member, of the *Good Autism Practice Journal*.

Maggie Bowen

Maggie gained her academic and professional qualifications at universities in Aberystwyth, Leeds and Bangor. She began her teaching career in a school for children with severe learning difficulties (SLD), and went on to work as a Community Liaison Teacher for individuals with SLD. She has been a Team Inspector of secondary and special schools and a Threshold Assessor, and has worked as part of a multi-agency team responsible for developing a range of new services for individuals of all ages with SLD.

She was Programme Leader for Special Educational Needs courses and the MA in Education at the North East Wales Institute of Higher Education (NEWI). She has worked for the Welsh Assembly Government as Development Officer for Inclusion in Wales with a specific responsibility for Autistic Spectrum Disorders (ASD), Able and Talented and SEN Training in Wales.

She joined the team at Autism Cymru as Head of Public and Voluntary Sector Partnerships/Deputy CEO in January 2005. She has published on a range of SEN issues in books and journals, and is still committed to training and consultancy work with a range of practitioners from health, social services, education, the criminal justice system and the emergency services.

Acknowledgements

Our sincere thanks go to a range of people who have helped us gather evidence for this book, namely all of the support workers we've ever worked with, members of the Autism Cymru Primary and Special Schools' Fora, colleagues on the Webautism Team (www.webautism.bham.ac.uk), Robert Hubbard at Priors' Court School, Jude Bowen and NoMAD.

How to use this book

This book is one in the series entitled 'The Autistic Spectrum Disorder Support Kit'. It focuses on the role of the support worker and the child or children with ASD that they support. The book looks at the basics of autistic spectrum disorders and the specific challenges that face the support worker in any school. Autism Cymru host a Forum for teachers and workers in primary, secondary and special schools, where they have the opportunity to share best practice but also their concerns about the young people in their care. The content of this book refers to some of the discussions that have taken place at these meetings and has therefore been shaped by the work of experienced practitioners.

Throughout the book readers are asked to examine issues from the perspective of the individual with ASD rather than adopt a traditional behavioural approach to the situation. Case studies of best practice and strategies suggested are designed to be of practical help to the reader. Readers are also given the opportunity to reflect on their practice and enhance their professional development by using the 'Reflective Oasis' sections contained in each chapter.

Note for readers

We have used the universal term 'support workers' to describe the workforce who daily operate alongside pupils with special educational needs in mainstream and special school classrooms. This is not meant to demean nor diminish the very important work that they do, but as we explore in Chapter 10, their title has had a long and varied history. Workforce regulations (2003) have created tiered levels of different titles and responsibilities, so we decided to put the nomenclature to the test with 20 special schools' teachers. The consensus was that there are over seven different job titles that one could use to describe the work. What everyone was in agreement with was the term *support* worker, which accurately describes most of the day-to-day activities. Therefore for ease of reference we are using the title 'support worker' to cover everyone who works in a classroom, on a salary and who is not the class teacher.

1

Autistic spectrum disorders basics

This chapter looks at the historical overview of the diagnosis of autistic spectrum disorders and the key defining features of the condition.

The condition of autistic spectrum disorders is one that has had an array of other names (most with the term 'autism' mentioned somewhere) throughout its relatively short diagnostic lifespan. The conditions of autism and also of Asperger syndrome were formally delineated in the mid-1940s by two separate Austrian medical practitioners: Leo Kanner, a child psychiatrist, and Hans Asperger, a paediatrician. This does not mean, however, that the condition has only existed since that time. It is possible that autism or its characteristics have existed through time, (Frith, 1989; Waltz, 2005).

Currently, we recognize the work of both Kanner, who described a set of characteristics, also termed Kanner's autism, classic autism (1943), and that of Asperger, who described similar characteristics and some physical differences. These two contemporaries published their research at around the same time, but by advantage of living in the USA, Kanner's work became known to the English-speaking population a long time before Asperger's, who published in Austria in German (1943), compared to an English account of Asperger's work by Wing, (1981). A fuller historical picture can be gained from reading Wing (1996), Frith (1989), Jordan (1999).

Over the last 60 years, their work has acted as a guide to crystallizing the condition of autistic spectrum disorders. The terminology has had a chequered history, from the time when it was assumed to be a temporary (in childhood) manifestation of mental illness, right through to some current terms which 'boggle our minds'.

Look at what professionals and others have used to describe ASD. These are all taken from literature and medical/educational notes.

What's in a name?

Kanner's autism
Classical autism
Childhood schizophrenia
Asperger (a hard sound for the 'g') syndrome
Autistic features
Childhood psychosis
Lack of theory of mind
Pathological demand avoidance
Idiot savant
Pervasive developmental disorder
Pervasive developmental disorder – NOS (Not Otherwise Specified)
Central coherence difficulties
Semantic pragmatic disorder
Executive function deficit

The current terminology is autistic (or autism) spectrum disorder/s (Wing, 1996). To have a basic understanding of the condition, it is important to know about the 'triad of impairments' (Wing, 1996) – the three main areas of development where people on the autistic spectrum manifest differences. These areas are social interaction, communication and rigidity of behaviour and thought.

Social interaction

- Preference for individual activities
- Apparent aloofness
- Indifference towards others
- More adult oriented than peer oriented
- Likely to exhibit different spontaneous responses
- Passive acceptance of contact
- Lack of empathy
- Failure to appreciate significant others
- Poor understanding of social rules and conventions
- Unable to seek comfort at times of distress

Wing and Gould (1978) believe that there is also a sub-group of three distinct character/behaviour types in social interaction.

Aloof

The most commonly manifest characteristic, which describe those people with ASD who behave as if you are not there, do not respond to your interactions and lead you to the place/activity that they want rather than requesting it.

Passive

May be the least common sub-group who are completely passive in their interactions with others/will accept interaction and become a willing 'participant' in whatever is happening.

Active but odd

These characteristics are evident in those who wish to have social contact but lack a means of initiating it in a socially appropriate way. So they may hold a gaze too long, sit too close or respond in an unpredictable way.

Communication

- Little desire to communicate socially
- Lack of understanding of non-verbal gestures of others
- Not appreciative of need to communicate information
- Idiosyncratic use of words and phrases
- Prescribed content of speech
- May talk *at* rather than *to*
- Poor grasp of abstract concepts and feelings
- Literal understanding of words and phrases
- Does not 'get' subtle jokes
- Will develop expression before understanding

Rigidity of behaviour and thought

- May have stereotyped play activities
- Can become attached to repetition of movement or certain objects/routines
- Complex order of play/activity
- Cannot deviate from one way of doing things
- May be tolerant of situations and then over-react to something minor
- May develop rituals that have to be completed
- Can have extreme physical rituals, e.g. spinning, rocking
- Can develop extreme behaviours to avoid certain stimuli

Areas of difference in the child's development have to be noted by the age of 3 years. This is not to say that diagnosis only happens in early childhood, but by reviewing early developmental milestones, a diagnostician will ask questions of parents/carers about their levels of communication and play *before* the age of 3.

The recognized descriptors for diagnosis are contained in two separate medical reference books: the *ICD 10 – International Classification of Diseases version 10* (1993), which is compiled by the World Health Organization, and the *DSM IV – Diagnostic and Statistical Manual of Mental Health version* IV (1994), which is compiled by the American Psychiatric Association.

REFLECTIVE OASIS

Do you recognize these characteristics in a child known to you?

How do these areas of impairment pervade the way they function?

What about children who do not have a diagnosis: are these characteristics evident in their functioning?

Here are some common characteristics of children with ASD in school:

Social interaction

Limited play skills
Limited peer tolerance
Inability to share or take turns
Inappropriate play or social behaviours
No desire to investigate or explore, unless it's an interest
Lack of empathy for others
Inability to know what others are thinking or feeling
Socially aloof or awkward
Restricted interests
Simple social actions are often a complicated process (lining up, personal space, dialogue)
May know some social conventions and apply them rigidly

Communication

Understands some basic instructions
Expresses own needs
Lack of desire to communicate
Lack of understanding of the attempts of others
No shared enjoyment of social situations
No use of gesture, intonation or non-verbal expression, and inability to understand their use by others
Cannot respond spontaneously
Appears not to 'hear' what has been said
Limited conversation repertoire
Talks incessantly on topic of interest and can manipulate conversations round to this topic

Rigidity of thought and behaviour

Does not understand pretend play/drama/role play
Cannot use imagination to create models or pictures – images are derived from others
Difficulty in social games – turn-taking, winning, a draw
Repetitive quality to play
Will copy but not necessarily understand – often sees the outcome (bad behaviour and punishment)
Inability to see cause and effect of their own behaviour
Holds black-and-white views
Doesn't understand subtlety/sarcasm/jokes
Cannot create spontaneously without a model or intensive input

Work by a Midlands special school (Aird and Lister, 1999) used these characteristics as an audit for ASD within their population of pupils with severe learning difficulties (SLD). Staff within the SLD field might be surprised to discover how many of these characteristics appear within many of their pupils. There is a general consensus of opinion that, in behavioural terms, there is no singular 'autistic' way of responding. These characteristics exist within all of us. The difference is that we, 'neurotypicals' (NTs) are very good at disguising our stress, anxieties and weaknesses. Those on the autistic spectrum are not.

Points to remember

- The use of different terminology
- The implications of the triad of impairments
- The relevance of ICD 10/DSM IV upon diagnosis

2

Facilitating inclusion

In this chapter the move towards Inclusive schools is charted over time and the specific issues around including a pupil with ASD are examined. The importance of managing transitions at any stage during a child's school life is looked at in detail with ideas and suggestions on how to make this as trouble-free as possible.

The trend towards more inclusion in schools was identified by the Salamanca Statement (UNESCO, 1994). Mainstream primary and secondary schools have increased the numbers of support staff employed as more and more pupils with disabilities are included. Research by Vincett, Thomas and Cremin (2005) has charted the exponential rise in the numbers of support staff in mainstream schools. Their study, in Essex, points to a two-fold increase overall of support assistants from 1997 to 2003 and during the same timeframe, a three-fold increase in secondary schools.

The Disability Discrimination Act (1995) requires *all* educational establishments to make adaptations to their buildings/provisions so that people with disabilities are not excluded. For many establishments this has entailed making physical adaptations to their environments. You may work in a building that has put in lifts or has ground-floor access for those pupils who cannot climb/descend stairs. These measures are often the first response to including more people with disabilities. Public perception is that disability is something that is visible and obvious.

This is not the case with ASD. Often the most visible sign is when something is seriously wrong and anxieties rise to the surface. This is particularly true among those with Asperger Syndrome, as their general demeanour does not usually give away their inner effort and turmoil. You may have had to try and explain to a colleague why Tommy has reacted in such an 'over the top' way when the teacher has loaded on additional instructions to do more work.

The heart of inclusion is allowing for, and respecting, the right to be different. This can go against the grain in schools where pupils are told 'You are not different to anyone else'. A supportive school will have dealt with difference, disability and personal strengths through its PSHE curriculum. This should exist in primary and special, as well as secondary, schools. Inclusion is a 'hearts and minds' issue. It challenges us to change our attitudes and expectations towards anyone with a disability.

Consider these excuses heard in real schools for not wanting to adapt teaching/provision to the needs of the child/ren with ASD:

'I can't treat him any different to the others ...'
'I have a class of 30 other pupils, it's not just him ...'
'The other children would start wanting the same considerations ...'
'I was not trained to teach this sort of child ...'

Fortunately, more schools are finding that by accepting, valuing and celebrating difference, their ethos has changed them into more supportive environments. Children recognize the strengths of each other, realize that they all cannot be good at everything and work well in supporting each other.

CASE STUDY

In topic work at the primary school where Joe attended, the teacher grouped children together according to the strengths that they had identified in circle time. In their topic on 'Forces' each group had five pupil members. Each member had a role within that group – one was a good writer, one was a good artist, one loved building and model-making, one was a good organizer and Joe was good at finding out facts and figures. He was given the task of looking at the reference books and surfing the Internet. He was able to find out more information on how forces are used in construction materials and came up with a good list of architectural structures that had used forces to their advantage.

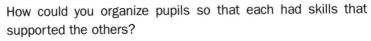

REFLECTIVE OASIS

How could you organize pupils so that each had skills that supported the others?

In what timetable areas could you undertake this sort of supportive group work?

How would you encourage a child with ASD to 'branch out' and use other skills and aptitudes?

It can be hard for a support worker to put forward suggestions to a teacher who is busy using all of the excuses not to include children. A steady 'drip, drip' approach may be needed. Try to find some allies among the school staff who can help get your messages across. You may be lucky and work in a staff group that is led by an inspirational head of department/headteacher. Capitalize on this to the advantage of the pupils whom you support.

Managing the transition from one school phase to another

Children with ASD often find changes very difficult to deal with. They may react strongly when changing from one activity to another. Others may work with the structured approach in the classroom, but have trouble with outside. In some schools at lunch-time, the additional pressure of queuing, choosing and paying for their food may be too much.

All of these transitions can be managed via a visual and structured approach with forward planning and anticipation (TEACCH – Treatment and Education of Autistic and Related Communication Handicapped Children, at the University of North Carolina **www.teacch.com**.). Greater transitions come when moving from one phase of education to the next. It is wise to plan ahead and become involved in the preparation for transition.

It has become the practice of many receiving schools to be introduced to the child/ren with ASD before they leave their first placement. Local primary schools serving and feeding into a larger secondary school have invited the SENCo or receiving head of department to the last annual review of the child who is moving on. Sometimes support workers are involved in this planning and will make a series of visits to the receiving school. It is quite common for the support worker to lose their contract once the child leaves and for a new support worker to be appointed in the receiving school. This has its advantages and disadvantages of course, but it has to be faced as a fact of life.

Schools and key personnel can use some very practical exercises in the British Institute of Learning Disabilities publication on transitions (BILD, 2005). Templates of useful transition documents containing valid information for key stakeholders in the process help to ensure that details are documented in one place. The book stresses that transitions will not just 'happen' to the child. There are some photocopiable resources for school staff to use that encourage the full and appropriate participation of the child. This will inevitably help you and the child to prepare for the new term at a new school. It is vital that sufficient information is not only received *before* the child joins the school but that the key people have read, understood and consulted on the documentation.

The support worker will be expected to translate the information and transform the factual detail into strategies. However, they can also be seen by colleagues as the person who is *responsible* for the child. This can be a huge pressure for someone who quite often is new to the school, new to the child and often finding their way in the world of ASD too. Other transition ideas are given by Salter and Twidle (2005).

CASE STUDY

One Midlands Inclusion Support Service has worked to prepare pupils for transition to their secondary school. They gather information on children with a diagnosis in their local authority and analyse secondary placements from year 7 to year 11 by criteria that may point to a potential breakdown. They believe one of the factors can be the late diagnosis of ASD.

They prioritize their work to include strategies that enable the pupil with ASD to feel supported in the transition process.
These include

- a sound transition plan
- devising a pupil passport
- playing board games that rehearse the transition
- colour coding of timetables and exercise books
- developing peer support systems
- work shadowing
- being involved in the child's transition from year 5 onwards.

(Cook and Stowe, 2003)

REFLECTIVE OASIS

How could you become more involved in preparing pupils for transition?

Could you approach the receiving school to pass on information?

What practical support, based on the ideas given above, could you contribute to the process?

Points to remember

- The Disability Discrimination Act 1995
- Recognising your pupils' strengths
- Developing strategies to manage change and transition across phases

How to build a strong working relationship with the pupil/s you support

We look at the specific skills and qualities that successful support workers employ when they are working with children with ASD. How to protect the child and promote their positive strengths in school are examined as well as the whole school issues of good lines of communication, staying in touch with parents and counteracting institutional discrimination.

When a new child with ASD enters your school, the support worker is often the first to get to know the child. You may have been involved in their admission to the school, visiting them at home or at their previous placement. Sometimes a child with ASD will join your school with a negative reputation – you may have heard 'stories' about them and what they are like. It is important that you give the child with ASD a 'clean slate'. This needs to be applied every day that they come into your school. Such is the nature of ASD that one cannot accurately predict the effects, positive or negative, that a new environment and new staff will have upon a child. Hopefully, your school will have as much information as possible about the child with ASD before they come. This, of course, is not always possible, but where you are able to plan a transition, you need to gain the fullest information, including from parents/carers *before* the child arrives.

Children with ASD are no different from other new pupils and they may have a muted or even a passive response to a new setting. This can sometimes last a day/week/term before the child feels settled in. Children with ASD may give an initial over-reaction to everything that is new and then they settle down. It cannot be stressed often enough that preparation and planning will help to pre-empt some initial difficulties. One important part of your role will be to act as an 'interpreter' for the child. Show how you can be relied upon to translate the requests made of the child and prove that you can be trusted and mean what you say. Many people with ASD say they respond to someone who sticks to their word and who acts in a reliable and predictable way. This is what they value in life.

Here are some ways in which you can prove yourself to them:

- Only make demands that you know they can achieve
- Use words sparingly, focus on conveying information visually
- Always be where you say you will be and at the time you have said
- Have a good way of letting them know when they have overstepped the mark
- Intervene and 'rescue' them if they are in difficulty
- Communicate with parents and show that you understand their child
- Always work out difficulties once the child is calm
- Mediate if they are being misunderstood
- Show them that they mean a lot to you – give them rewards that they appreciate (e.g. extra computer time, the chance to do classroom tidying, getting them a comic they like)

How to be the champion of the child

Once you have their trust and appreciation, you will be their 'champion'. Without the belief of someone else in us, few of us would achieve what we do in life. If all you got in your life were negatives and criticisms and you were surrounded by people who thought you were no good, your self-esteem would be low.

We all need someone who holds our best interests at heart. They will be honest and give constructive criticism and point you in the right direction. People with ASD need this too. We receive them being honest with us: 'Miss, your hair looks a mess today' and we need to have the same truthfulness in our dealings with them: 'You need to wash your armpits and wear deodorant'.

By being explicit with them and telling what is needed you are helping them to make that adjustment independently – if we held our noses or were sarcastic, the message would not be clear for them.

CASE STUDY

Ellie was a young woman of 15 years. She joined the school after an unsuccessful placement elsewhere. Her teacher and support worker had visited her previous placement, talked to her parents, spent time observing her doing what she enjoyed doing best – sifting and sorting strips of paper. Ellie had been taught how to use the Picture Exchange Communication System (PECS; Bondy and Frost, 1994) to make basic requests. Parents talked to the staff about the sorts of things that Ellie could do independently. They arranged for Ellie to make half-day visits to the school and the classroom before she started there full-time. Ellie was given labelled digital images of her classroom, the teacher and support worker and important places around the school (e.g. the toilets, the dining room) to take home with her.

Before Ellie started school she had a visual schedule of what was going to happen during the first day and who was going to be there to meet her at the front of the school. By having visual schedules of each day's events, Ellie could rely upon the information and so transitions and activities outside of the classroom were not a surprise to her. The support worker used the PECS system to ensure that Ellie initiated requests and was given understandable information. When Ellie had had enough, the support worker intervened and gave her a chance to de-stress by sifting and sorting paper. This was also her reward for tasks completed.

Ellie and the support worker became good 'friends' in a short space of time. On several occasions others interpreted Ellie's actions as negative and the support worker put 'Ellie's side of things'. Sometimes other pupils revised their negative view of Ellie. Her parents were able to ask the school to help them out with transferable skills (e.g. dealing with menstruation). Although Ellie progressed up through the school and left her first support worker behind, she always made a point of coming to say 'Hello' everyday.

REFLECTIVE OASIS

How do you presently work to build up a relationship with a new child?

How far are you able to be involved in the transition from a previous placement?

Recall a child who remembered you long after you stopped working with them. Why do you think you made a long-lasting impression upon them?

Skills for protecting the pupil

Once you have become the champion of the child/ren you are working with, colleagues may rely upon you to do all of the interaction with the child. This is often seen in mainstream classrooms where the teacher has the responsibility of the whole class – maybe up to 30 or more other children who can learn pretty much at the pace set. The effect of being the child's 'champion' can be a double-edged sword – you can build upon a feeling of continuity and security but, conversely, every time the child cannot cope with the conformity of being in class, colleagues look to you to 'deal with it'. Sometimes blame can be transferred from child to adult – 'Oh, Mrs C could not control John so we had to come back from our trip'. You may feel de-skilled by such remarks.

Lines of communication have to be kept open so that your colleagues do not take on such attitudes. If you express a willingness to help to plan and make resources for lessons, suggest that sometimes it would be a good exchange for the teacher to work with the child with ASD (to build their own relationship) and for you to be in charge of the bigger group. The child/ren with ASD do need structure and consistency in their lives, but they do not need someone to be their sole carer, educator and company for the whole day.

If negativity is being expressed directly or indirectly towards the child by adults at school, this needs to be challenged. Open negativity will have to be addressed head-on. Where the negativity stems from misunderstanding of the condition of ASD, regard yourself as a valuable resource. Point people to where they can find out more factual information about ASD. Use materials and experiences that you have found valuable. Maybe there's someone on the staff of the school who has direct experience/resources that they could share. Often a colleague will either know of a person with ASD or be a parent themselves. Make them an ally to help to protect the child you are working with. Where the child is being addressed with sarcasm or irony, a gentle word about people with ASD not generally understanding subtleties of language may be appropriate.

For the child with ASD to have to endure open negativity from their peers is a whole-school issue. The way in which we treat others and the respect that is needed for everyone, regardless of their disability, needs to be on the school's agenda. Disrespect by another child needs an immediate response to stop such action from growing through direct or indirect permission. Resorting to put-downs disrespects the offender. Closer questions might get to the bottom of their behaviour. This type of incident needs reporting wider as it represents a form of bullying.

CASE STUDY

Matthew, a Year 9 boy, came home from school one day and said he'd made several new friends. Matthew said his friends were funny, laughed a lot and invited him to join in with their game. His mum was happy for him. The 'games' that Matthew's friends played included throwing his coat outside the school railings and into mud; flicking ink/paint at him and making up sexual stories about him. These things happened at break time when he was not with his support worker.

Matthew had mistakenly believed that because other pupils knew his name and called him over to be with them, then they must be his 'friends'. He did not predict that they would try to ruin his possessions, nor did he understand the innuendo and sexual connotations of their stories.

REFLECTIVE OASIS

Does the child with ASD that you work with have an idea about who friends are and how they should behave?

How might you introduce the topic of friends and bullies to them?

Is it necessary for your school to consider providing more support at social times?

Counteracting institutional discrimination

We all bring our own expectations, attitudes, experiences and skills into our workplace. Traditional practices such as corporal punishment, gender inequality, discrimination of religion have been made against the law. We should not have to work in a climate that permits any of these practices.

Inequality and the way in which difference is viewed is a whole-school issue and a named member of staff should act as a resource/adviser in these matters. As a member of staff you will need to know who to go to when you have concerns over issues of the policies, practices and ethos of the school discriminating openly – this is institutional discrimination. If you are not satisfied by their response or the action taken, then it needs to go to a higher authority.

Where the discrimination involves a disability – either by omission (e.g. forgetting to include someone in a wheelchair) or commission (e.g. not allowing the child to take part because of their disability) it needs tackling by whole-school training. If the child with ASD is discriminated against – then as their champion, you will need to raise it. In counteracting institutional discrimination against disability there is no more powerful a message to be given than by a person with that disability. Use speakers with ASD like Wendy Lawson or Ros Blackburn to talk to staff; or there are TV programmes that can be taped/hired that will put across the view of the person with ASD.

Keeping in touch with home

When they get home, the child with ASD is likely to say 'nothing' happened at school when asked by the parent/carer, because they may find it hard to retain a memory of relevant events. This is why some system of keeping in touch with home is of vital importance. It should be a reciprocal process so that you will know of any events in the child's home life. Many schools run a home/school diary where details of events can be recorded and passed between those two bases. This system works well if there is a commitment on both sides to keep it up.

Many schools profess to having an 'open-door policy' when it comes to receiving visits from parents or responding to them on the telephone. Often that is contradictory to what they actually do. Here are some typical ways of putting people off:

The school secretary fields all calls and promises 'Someone will phone you back'

'I can't find Mr H, call back at lunch time/end of school'

'Miss K is teaching now and cannot come to the phone'

Often calling back is not convenient either. When communicating with parents it can helpful to specify periods of the day or particular days when you could be interrupted or can be available to take a phone call.

Other ways to have a flow of communication with home could take the form of short videos or digital photo attachments, personal contact every time the child has done something highly commendable, telephone pictures with mobile phone technology – these would capture the 'exact moment', a weekly class newsletter. A support worker and parent of a child with ASD at the Autism Cymru Primary School Forum meeting recommended a 'Talking photo album' (www.liberator.co.uk) – digital or photographic images could be put into the pocket-holder with a short commentary. Discussion with parents will help alleviate their concerns over how and when to get in touch.

Points to remember

- Take time to get to really know your pupils
- Find ways to gain their trust and champion their cause
- Raise awareness of your pupils' needs among staff and other pupils
- Develop good home–school links

Working with differing learning styles

This chapter highlights the different ways in which we all learn, and spends time looking at some of the specific areas that a child with ASD may use their senses to learn. Finding out how the child that you support learns is examined, and support workers are encouraged to find ways to build upon learning modality to the advantage of the child.

A current educational trend is that we need to match up how different people learn with how they are taught. This has expanded the view in schools that not only is it important what the children learn (teaching content) but also how they learn it. Research by Coffield, Moseley, Hall and Ecclestone (2004) found around 70 theories of learning style, published from 1902 to 2002. Their extensive critique has led them to cautiously conclude that using learning styles as the major component of teaching limits the scope and content *and* the motivation of the learner. They would advise that learning styles are not the be all and end all of what is taught and how it is learnt.

The major strands in the research on learning styles done by the Coffield *et al.* (2004) focus on three principal modes of learning:

Visual – information taken in and processed by the eyes – 'Show me (in a picture) what to do and I'll do it'
Auditory – information taken in and processed by the ears – 'Tell me what to do and I'll do it'
Kinaesthetic – information taken in and processed by the body – 'Walk me through what to do and I'll do it'

Most of us use all three ways to varying degrees and in different circumstances. One way of finding out what type of learner someone is is to note how they tackle 'self-assembly' furniture. Do they:

- Read the instructions and look at the diagrams (visual)?
- Respond when you read the instructions and tell them where pieces go (auditory)?
- Need to take apart a similar piece of furniture to understand where everything goes (kinaesthetic)?

These are ways of picking up on someone's learning style but, as Coffield *et al.* (2004) conclude, there are no particularly sensitive or reliable ways of determining style.

As much as 99 per cent (Walker Tileston, 2004) of our information about the world and our experiences come from a sensory source. In school environments, children take in instructions, directions and information auditorily. Auditory overload can happen in schools too – think of the level of noise in the play area or canteen. You may remember instances when words were not enough to help you to establish a concept. Think how something like 'Forces' in science can be better understood by engaging in pushing, pulling and resistance activities.

A guide to ways in which we learn

Visual learners

This is probably the most common style. Use of the chalkboard/overhead projector/Smart screen assists visual learners. Video, DVD and computers have brought many complex concepts/topics into our classrooms.

Visual learners can often be spotted by the following characteristics (Walker Tileston, 2000):

- Not good at people's names but remembers things about them
- Learns best when the teaching is accompanied by visual tools
- Likes to read themselves, rather than listen to a story
- Writes down their thoughts to memorize and organize them – use mind maps and spider diagrams
- Likes visual pastimes – jigsaws, computers

Auditory learners

Auditory learners are the smallest proportion of students. For some auditory learners, the memory of what they have heard is retained in the brain in the sequence given and has to be retrieved in that same sequence too. For example; learning multiplication tables by rote and having to recite the tables to get to the required answer:

'What are 7 eights?'
'1 eight is 8, 2 eights are 16, 3 eights are 24, 4 eights are 32, 5 eights are 40, 6 eights are 48, aaah 7 eights are 56'

This can have its advantages as a form of recall but can be time-consuming. Problems arise when the question does not contain the same language or format as the item to be retrieved. Auditory learners can often be spotted by the following characteristics (Walker Tileston, 2000):

- Easily put off by external noises
- Make good raconteurs and story-tellers
- Like to speak their report rather than read it
- Are good at remembering names
- Forget what they have read until asked to talk about it
- Like physical rewards – clapping, patting, hugging
- Can be affected by room comfort factors – too bright, too hot, too loud

Kinaesthetic learners

Kinaesthetic learners need to move around. They are the students who fidget/squirm/use the slightest excuse to get out of their places (crossing the room for each separate item). Kinaesthetic learners often get a bad press in traditional classrooms because they can be so active and possibly disruptive. Physical experiences are what they crave and concepts that have involved movement are what they hold onto and retain.

Kinaesthetic learners can often be spotted by the following characteristics (Walker Tileston, 2000):

- Retain what was done, not what was said or heard
- Their problem-solving tends to be physical
- Like to join in, rather than watch
- Enjoy physical pursuits, drama, rehearsal and role playing
- Enjoy making models
- Let their emotions show through their body language

Common differences in ASD

These three ways of learning – *learning modalities* – encapsulate the majority of learners in any one situation. Current popular approaches for people with ASD (e.g. TEACCH – www.teacch.com; PECS – www.pecs.org.uk) will tap into the widely held belief that they are predominantly visual learners. We must guard against thinking that all people with ASD learn visually. There is still so much to know about how people on the spectrum learn and retrieve information and we have been helped by the accounts of Grandin (1995a, b), Williams (1992, 1996) and Lawson (2005). Lawson divides learning styles into our neurotypical (NT) polytropic (many sensory channels) processing and the ASD monotropic (single-channel) style. She talks about how NT people can focus on more than one thing happening while they are taking in information; so they:

- can understand information that is not formed into a complete sentence (Les Dawson and Roy Barraclough over the garden fence)
- can read intention and subtlety
- can make connections while processing the information and draw similarities and conclusions – (people who finish off the sentence for you)
- can automatically retrieve other items from memory ('that reminds me of....)
- can be walking, swimming or dancing while all of this is going on
- can cope with change (cancellations are quickly put into perspective)

Wendy Lawson is not the only person with ASD who says that looking and listening at the same time are incredibly difficult. We often take looking as a guaranteed sign of listening. Or we insist that the child looks at us before we deliver the instruction. If we are wearing an overpowering scent/have changed our hairstyle, then the chances of the child being able to extract what is most important are slight.

Lawson says the person with ASD may be receiving information or learning new concepts in different ways:

- The tendency to understand in a literal way might interfere with the exact meaning that you intend – 'let's go and paint a picture with a partner' (not with paint?)
- Not seeing how things could be connected in meaning and action – the life cycle of a dolphin as a mammal will be the same as other mammals
- Not understanding social rules may make social conventions hard to teach and learn – turn-taking; speaking and listening; taking a guess

Grandin (1995b) says that when someone talks about a dog, she describes having a 'drop-down menu' of all of the dogs she has known in her lifetime before she can process what is being said about *this* dog.

Finding the modality and capitalizing on the way the child learns

Information should be taken from parents on how they have witnessed their son/daughter processing new experiences/information. You can look at what the child is doing when a new task/instruction is presented to them. Use the VAK (visual, auditory, kinaesthetic) characteristics to ascertain how the child is responding. Communication symbols from the Picture Exchange Communication System (Bondy and Frost, 1994) use the visual aspect of learning to communicate – sequencing individual cards containing 'I want' statements into whole sentences. The TEACCH (Mesibov, Shea and Schopler, 2004) approach uses clear visual information to help structure progression towards independent work habits and everyday routines. Both approaches have been shown to work well with many with ASD. They can be starting points for children who are struggling to get meaning from classroom activities. If the child that you work with can talk, they may still need the scaffold of a communication system to help them to understand how and why people converse.

Visual learners will be good at making diagrams, pictures, graphs and other visual representations of their ideas; auditory learners will be good at retaining stories, rhymes and mnemonics; kinaesthetic learners will be able to make constructions, act out and develop working models of their designs. Each modality has a positive aspect that can be allowed to flourish and progress within every classroom. The key is to find the preferred/predominant modality, work on those strengths but also incorporate aspects of the other modalities too.

Points to remember

- Consider teaching and learning styles
- Examine your use of language from the perspective of your pupils with ASD
- Find out how your pupils with ASD process and react to new information/experiences

5

Working with sensory differences

This chapter looks at the contribution of 7 senses to the common sensory differences of the person with ASD. Practical suggestions and hints are made to try to alleviate some of the more acute differences that people with ASD report.

People with ASD have contributed much to our insight into sensory differences (Williams, 1992, 1996; Lawson, 2000; Grandin, 1995a, b). They report that all of their senses can at some time be affected by distortions and disturbances, making their experiences very different from ours.

Consider the average birthday party and its sensory stimulation:

- Overexcited children
- An array of tempting food
- Loud party games
- Balloons
- Presents and present wrappings
- Unpredictable movements
- Games, prizes and winning
- Not knowing when it's going to end

Now consider how you might feel if you liked sameness, familiarity, clear boundaries and rules, certainty and not too much noise. The experience must be uncomfortable. Added to this, the social context may not be understood.

Common sensory differences

First-person authors have explained how their senses can distort the incoming sensory information. Prior to their explanations, few people knew how things could appear quite different for them. Here are some ways in which sensory differences may impinge upon the child in your school.

Visual

Visual distortions

Some say that their sight can give them the perception that everything is tapering down in dimension or that things look longer/bigger/smaller/ shorter than they actually are. Most will say that this is not a perpetual way of perceiving the world.

Others find it hard to focus directly on things and prefer to use squinted eyes or the edge of their eyes – peripheral vision. Dyslexia is a common condition with ASD and pupils you are working with may have been prescribed coloured filters – Irlen lenses (**www.irlen.com**) – with their reading.

Useful strategies

- Try checking different coloured filters and see if there is a particular preference.
- Watch their free play. Often children with ASD are subtly telling us what they prefer.
- Be aware of when a child will refuse to enter a setting: it may be their expression of a dislike of lighting or humidity or temperature.

Visual likes and dislikes

You may know a child who likes stationery lined up in a certain order, or who will use only some colours. They are probably unable to explain, but they may be very resistant to suggested change. Always consider strong visual likes and dislikes. Work towards extending and enhancing their experiences.

Useful strategies

- Look carefully at recurring patterns/themes in free play and their schoolwork. Incorporate their patterning and colour sequences into a valued skill – let them design a part of a display or coloured containers for pens/pencils.

- If tidying obstructs learning, then find a time and place. Tidiness is something we can all value in children – make them into a monitor for the classroom.
- Simple visual instructions to show when they can get to tidy (always after completing a task or at a set time of day).
- Teach 'a time and a place'. Once they can see that what they want to do is a *reward*, they can relax.

Auditory

Hearing anomalies

It is hard to know whether what you have said has been heard by the child with ASD. Often they do not respond to loud repetitive sounds (e.g. pneumatic drills) but can become distressed by smaller, quieter noises (a computer's fan). They might love certain phrases or narrate a whole Disney video, including the speech tones/inflexions that they would not normally use. Most have a very acute sense of hearing. A child holding their fingers over their ears or partially covering the outer ear is a sign that their auditory sense is overloaded. Many find music relaxing. Use of personal stereos or MP3/iPods can help in overriding noise distress. It is also an effective and socially acceptable coping strategy.

Useful strategies

- Forewarn of the event – if you know there is going to be a fire practice, let them know.
- Suggest some simple ways of drowning out the noise (the iPod idea).
- Many secondary schools have used inventive ways of acclimatizing children with ASD to the end-of-lesson bell.
- Try to analyse why the child may be having distortions in their hearing.

Tactile

Tactile defensiveness

Many say that firm holds and grasps are preferable to lighter stroking. If the child prefers no touch at all, we have to respect that. You may have a child who likes to engage in a ritual like 'Tig' – when you touch them, they have to return the touch.

Useful strategies

- These can be entrenched reactions, which may not be improved by our intervention. It is worth trying sensory desensitization to build up tolerance levels.

- Identify their strong dislikes.
- Introduce activities that contain elements of their defensiveness.
- Replicate ways in which close proximity may be needed in other activities. Try blindfolding them, so that others can guide them around.
- If you work on identifying what type of touch they prefer, build up times for using it.
- The game of 'Tig' is a popular playground game that could be enjoyed by children with ASD.

Tactile intolerance

Not only do they find some touches hard to tolerate, they also find some textiles uncomfortable. This may include not being able to wear certain fabrics, like wool and other itchy textiles, or finding the feel of cuffs or manufacturer's labels in the side seams of garments intolerable. A lot of people with ASD prefer to wear what they call 'least restrictive clothing' i.e. soft cotton clothing with no tightness or seams.

You may also come across those who like to be tightly buttoned into their clothing because this represents a physical feeling of security to them.

It is quite common to find children who are absolutely fastidious about not getting dirty and will wash their hands over and over again. Conversely, you might find children who glory in getting as mucky as possible.

Useful strategies

- The variety of textiles and fabrics available, styles and fastenings make it easier to buy what the person with ASD can tolerate. Materials like linen and cotton are easily available.
- Fastenings like Velcro and press-studs may make it easier for the child with ASD to be independent.
- Information from home will guide on types of clothing, preferred fabrics and whether labels need removing before the child wears new clothes.

Olfactory and gustatory

Taste/smell predominance

People with ASD are likely to have developed some strong preferences for food types, often focusing on foods with distinctive tastes (like Marmite and curries) or particular textures (crispy, smooth). It may be difficult to introduce new taste experiences, but persevere and ring the changes as each step is achieved. Do not deprive them of their preferred food as the child may refuse to eat anything during school time. You may come across someone who insists on tasting any new materials or smelling everything. Providing the taste or smell is not going to upset/poison them, this should be permitted. Where the exploration by taste or smell is dangerous, respond in a way that the child knows means 'No' or actively prohibit them doing so.

Useful strategies

- Note smell preferences and use as a relaxant – like essential oils or toiletry items.
- Persevere and take advice from home for taste preferences and restricted diets.
- If a child is actively searching out food, think about how to provide small amounts of food at regular times.

Other sensory considerations

We automatically think of the five senses, but work by occupational therapists (Ayres, 1979) and a psychiatrist (Hinder, 2004) identify two other senses that help us to process the world. Proprioception/proxemics and vestibular are both gross motor (whole-body) receptors. Proprioception/proxemics is the way in which we position ourselves in space and time and know how to keep a suitable distance from others. This will include what is a suitable distance from those we know and also from those who are strangers. Vestibular is our innate sense of balance and knowing our capacities in exploring new experiences.

Proprioception and proxemics

Differences in proprioception and proxemics may affect the positioning of the body in space, strength of grasp and the amount of awareness the person with ASD has of objects, furniture and people around them. Although people with ASD have a very fixed, albeit invisible, boundary around themselves, they are no respecter of other people's personal space. They may get close to any person that they perceive can fulfil a need for them. This makes them particularly vulnerable when out in public.

Useful strategies

- Work with them to recognize the boundaries that they themselves apply and then transfer that consideration to others. Using the distance of an arm's length is a good guide, although this is best practised at home or at school!

- If you are working with someone who actively invades your and other people's space, you may need to include something more visual and concrete to them.
- Use a smell identity and try sticking to one particular perfume to teach 'Close enough, I know you'.
- Use tape/visual markers on the floor, like actors use stage markings to know where to stand.
- A quoit or a laminated coloured cross can be thrown on the floor as the child begins their communication with you.
- Use a social story (Gray, 2000) to illustrate what is close enough and too close. Use of humour or rhymes will appeal to many children.

Vestibular

Do you know a child who:

loves physical exploration
climbs to the highest point as a lookout
balances on even the thinnest surfaces?

This ability is linked to their vestibular sense and they appear to lack fear of danger or falling even when in the most precarious position.
What about children who:

love spinning
enjoy rocking, hanging upside down and swinging
persistently go on fairground rides such as the 'Waltzers'?

These children are seeking out experiences that give them an extreme sensory high. Try joining in: you could find that they do give an adrenaline burst that leaves you feeling good!

Useful strategies

- PE lessons give opportunities to scale reasonable heights and hang and swing upside-down. Well-equipped schools (often secondary or special schools) have trampolining equipment – this encourages daring moves within a safe environment.
- Parents have found rebounders or trampettes useful.

- Your school may consider providing space hoppers or pogo sticks for all children.
- Take them to climbing walls and outdoor centres, provided you have risk-assessed the activity and are able to have a qualified instructor.
- Daily Life Therapy (Kitahara, 1984) uses aerobic exercise as a means of preparing children to settle down to work. The endorphins released by exercise acts as a de-stressor to the children (and adults) too.

The good-practice pointers (DfES, 2002) acknowledge that sensory differences deserve our consideration. In practical terms, be aware that:

- A noisy room may cause distress
- Instructions to the whole group may be ignored by the child with ASD.
- An instruction prefaced with their name, 'Andrew, you need to…' makes it obvious who you are talking to
- Anxiety about belongings and furniture may effectively rule out their concentration for the whole session
- If the teaching medium is oral – the learning medium is auditory – sensory differences may preclude understanding – use visual back-up
- Simple instructions may baffle – 'let's go and wash our hands in the toilet'
- The person may need an obvious structure within which to function

---

CASE STUDY

Gary, a 13-year-old boy with ASD and additional learning difficulties, attends a special school for children with ASD. He spits, bites, pinches and kicks anyone near him when he is feeling stressed. He is very strong and has needed restraining in the past.

The support staff decided to observe and monitor his outbursts and collected four weeks' data. A functional analysis indicated Gary not being able to make sense of what was being said to him because of background noise in the playground, the hall, lunchtimes and PE. The response to Gary feeling stressed by noise was physically to 'shut him down'. Gary was quite tactile defensive and he perceived this as physical assault, causing further reactive responses. Analysis showed that where physical restraint had been applied, the holds required more and more adults. Gary took the rest of the day to calm down.

(Continued)

The staff considered:

- Sensory overload during Gary's day. Gary was shadowed for a day and the stimulation from hearing and touch senses was examined.
- Sometimes even a 'quiet' environment over-stimulated him and he made his own noises to fill the void. He could tolerate a low 'hum' of noise and activity in his classroom.
- Structure and routines were introduced to make the environment predictable and easier to control.
- Gary was given 'stop and go' cards – red for stop and green for go – to indicate when things were getting too much. It took several weeks of dedicated work by the staff and a resolution to obey the colour of the card. Peers had to learn too.
- A hands-off approach was used when he started to 'lose it'.
- The red and green cards became a form of communication – staff and peers were able to show Gary a red card when things were getting too much.
- Gary was taught ways to calm himself down, including deep breathing, arm-folding, temple massaging and using a visual symbol to ask for time alone.

From a case study by Olga Bogdashina for the webautism course (2003) (by kind permission of the author)

REFLECTIVE OASIS

List some of the ways in which the child/ren you work with use their senses to gain information

List how they spend their free time and whether this fulfils a sensory function for them

How could you use their sensory preferences to present new tasks?

Points to remember

- Consider the full range of sensory differences
- Examine the school environment and timetable in relation to sensory issues
- Use sensory preferences to maximize learning

Observing and record-keeping

We examine the value of observing and keeping records and ways in which this can be done. Instances of inappropriate/challenging behaviours are used to illustrate three different forms of recording, and each approach is analysed for its advantages and disadvantages. The concept of behaviour being a communication is raised and explored, with the encouragement to look for the message.

Why observe?

It is often the case that your success in supporting a pupil with ASD is not only down to the relationship you have developed with them, but also how much time you can spend observing them and then having time to reflect on what that has taught you. It is as important to observe a pupil within a formal teaching setting in a lesson as watching them when they are out and about in school during social times. If you can record breaktime information in some way, then it will serve as a valuable record to share with others, including their parents. Observation helps us to compose a rounded picture of the child and for those with ASD this will be invaluable in your support of them.

A continuous record, a 'reflective log' will have dates and times of what you have observed. An exercise book with margins drawn to make it easier to assemble and organize your thoughts will do. If you detect a pattern in your observations, then you could organize the layout more to make columns for ticks of a particular habit/behaviour.

Brookfield (1995) says that if we develop a theory about a child or an event, we justify the action arising from it. Consider the child who screams in the changing room when going swimming (which he loves). Over time colleagues have put the behaviour down to an 'off-day' which justified it being an isolated event. However, this continues. Perhaps we conclude that he no longer likes swimming? So we ban taking him for a few weeks.

If the reason for the screaming is the change of lighting in the changing room, how can the end justify the means? Brookfield calls this 'unchecked common sense'. We need to test our theory against the possible reasons and then evaluate which one holds true.

Brookfield (1995) states

> Ten years of practice can be one years' worth of distorted experience repeated ten times. The 'experienced' teacher may be caught with self-fulfilling interpretative frameworks that remain closed to any alternative perspectives, (p7)

If we develop the habit of observing, recording and reflecting upon the experiences of the child and our own perspectives, we have a better chance of being more accurate about our assumptions.

If we are stuck in a rut with a child, we may think that there is someone 'out there' who can help with a new perspective/skills. They may have a different way of looking at things, but you are often the person who can make the difference and implement their suggestions.

Using observation and recording for incidents of challenging behaviour

Quite often schools claim to have 'tried everything' in attempting to shape behaviours. These attempts are frequently based on what our theory about the behaviour is; that it could be 'learned behaviour' or 'copycat behaviour'. These theories fit our personal constructs and our attempts to intervene are influenced by what we think is at the core. If we want to thoroughly investigate this, we must determine how, why and when these behaviours occur. This is where structured recording and observation is needed.

All three following systems of record-keeping are retrospective, not contemporaneous – they are filled in after the sequence of events has occurred. You should complete them as soon as you can after the incident to ensure accuracy.

ABC records

One of the most familiar retrospective recording systems is the use of 'ABC charts' (Presland, 1989), with the three letters standing for:

A – Antecedents – what has led up to the incident

B – Behaviour – an objective record of what behaviours were observed

C – Consequences – what has happened after the behaviour.

This type of recording once the incident has finished is commonly employed to help to identify/analyse behaviours that are both challenging and persistent.

One of the most efficient uses of ABC data is to determine a short period of data collection and then do a thorough analysis. ABC recording is very useful in helping to pinpoint specific antecedents like the sequence of actions (triggers) that lead up to an incident.

The ABC recording system will not reduce behaviours if it is

- Only completed by one person
- Done long after the event
- Gathering dust in a child's file and not referred to
- Not part of individual planning.

STAR

Zarkowska and Clements (1994) have looked at the significance of the setting. The STAR approach was first developed for people with severe learning difficulties (including those with ASD) and it focuses on the:

S – Setting – the environment where the challenging behaviour took place, including presence of others and activity

T – Trigger – the events/sequence of actions that have set the behaviour off

A – Action – what the person actually does in response

R – Results – what happens after the behaviour and what function of the behaviour is for that person.

The STAR approach promotes factual, objective recording. Its focus helps us to consider other factors which may be influencing the behaviour of a person with ASD. However, its effectiveness is limited by the same factors as the ABC approach.

8 step

The work of specialist educational psychologist Whitaker (2001), the 8-step system expands upon the STAR approach and uses its features in an 8-step plan.

The 8 steps begin with the collective decision of where to start, which is often the hardest thing to do when working with a child who has a range of equally difficult behaviours.

After dealing with the components of settings, triggers, actions and results, the 8 steps conclude with the decision of how to prevent incidents, how to teach new skills and behaviours and how to make the function of the behaviour less of a reward.

When trying to intervene in a situation that is escalating into a major incident, Whitaker (2001) suggests trying the following:

- Remove the identified trigger
- Respond to the behaviour as a communication
- Distract
- Remind person of reward
- Remind person of 'rules'
- Provide opportunity to 'chill out'
- Restate the request
- Small change to request/scale it down
- Calm things down.

If the incident continues to escalate, then personal safety of the individual, others and yourself assumes priority. Whitaker recommends:

- Making the environment safe
- Removing others for their safety if needed
- Requesting/calling for help
- Giving a low-key response
- Using a physical intervention with other staff, as a last resort and adopting strategies you have been trained in and know how to use as a team.

Once the escalation has calmed down, remember that the adrenaline produced by the event may take up to two hours to subside. This is why, when things become calmer, they can suddenly flare up again. Give them time, without pressure to regain their own control. Once the recovery phase begins, remember to:

- Give space
- Try and restore normality to the situation
- Calmly restate your demands

- Talk the situation through, if possible
- Seek support from other staff with the individual and also for yourself.

Whitaker states that the 8-step plan helps us to:

- Systematically organize our thoughts and observations
- Look at the underlying function of the behaviour for the person exhibiting it
- Divert challenging behaviours
- Form a commitment for acting upon incidents that challenge us and helps us to resolve issues.

The advantage of this system is that it promotes teamwork with several people involved in the decision of where to start and then it builds through more team involvement in response and shaping new behaviours.

Behaviour as communication

Any form of extreme behaviour is 99 per cent a means of communicating something for the individual with ASD. We have to pay attention to the message it conveys or the behaviour will not be moderated. We need to try and fathom out what function the behaviour is serving for them, e.g. do they get removed from a situation they don't want to be in? Does it get rid of people they don't like?

We need to bear in mind the situation the child is in and:

- Collect the perceptions of parents/carers – is the behaviour well established, does it occur with them, how do they respond?
- Reframe the way in which the behaviour is viewed by us/others. Is it always viewed as attention-seeking?
- Focus upon how it could be shaped into something more acceptable and appropriate.
- Remember a positive approach to the person and their behaviour is likely to achieve a better result and is more humane.
- Think creatively to teach the individual an acceptable way of achieving the same end result, e.g. using a red/green symbol to let us know when their stress levels and tolerance are OK/near to explosion.

Remember that strategies which only react to the behaviour (e.g. physical intervention) should be short-term. But also remember that 'challenging behaviour' is not simple or speedy to change.

- Retrospectively analyse the behaviour and consequences – looking for the other reasons for challenging behaviour – is it illness, poor sleeping patterns, diet, lack of communication skills?

- Teach replacement skills alongside ways in which the child can identify the build-up of tensions
- Teach ways in which they can effectively calm themselves – counting to 10 or using de-stressing toys – squeeze balls, etc.

Finally, treat the behaviour as a form of communication – if the pupil could articulate what they felt at that particular point, what would they be saying?

CASE STUDY

Robert with ASD in Year 10 had developed a reputation for being difficult to manage. The teacher's view of him was that he was academically weak. He attended the resource base set up in the school and saw a specialist for his behaviour for 30 minutes every week. Closer observation of Robert revealed that when he was on task he was more academically able than had been presumed.

In discussion with Robert, it was decided to focus upon behaviours. Robert appreciated the interest shown in him and it was suspected that he was also suffering from very low self-esteem.

A behaviour-monitoring plan and classroom achievement record were devised and targets were negotiated and agreed by Robert with his signature. This plan was shared with all of Robert's subject teachers. Four areas were chosen to be the focus of his performance in each lesson:

- Level of independence
- Behaviour
- Attention to task
- Completion of task

Visual aids and back-up instructions were provided for Robert to be as independent as possible.

Each area was rated on a scale from 1 to 5, with 1 being Poor and 5 being Excellent.

(Continued)

Two members of support staff covered his time in school and they met at breaktimes to share their findings. Teaching staff were informed about the recording plan and were asked not to intervene in a behavioural incident, unless requested to do so by the support staff.

When Robert became anxious about the pressure to conform and achieve, he was taught how to use de-stressing techniques, such as deep breathing, and he had the use of a quiet room to calm down by himself. The support workers enabled Robert to develop an awareness of the escalation of stress inside himself and also provided him with a vocabulary of new emotion words so that he could articulate how he was feeling.

A year later, Robert is attending 52 per cent of classes independently and is now able to recognize and articulate the signs of stress within himself. He is achieving his academic potential and is expected to pass at least four GCSEs.

He came to be considered as an enthusiastic pupil making a good effort, bright and polite. His self-control is considered to be at the level where he can be trusted to take part in a work experience placement in his local community.

(From case study details contributed Denise Hawkins, Argoed School, Flintshire)

REFLECTIVE OASIS

In what ways could you work to systematically collect data on a child's performance?

Would you be able to involve the child in agreeing to the collection of such information?

How would you go about teaching a child with ASD to recognize the signs of stress?

Points to remember

- Take time to observe your pupils and record findings
- Use methods like ABC, STAR and the 8-step plan to eliminate challenging behaviour
- Behaviour is a means of communication – so look for the message!

7

Building self-esteem

This chapter deals with the importance of accentuating the positive strengths of the child with ASD and looks at ways in which these can be built upon and employed for the benefit of all. Individual Education Plans; self advocacy and dealing with bullies is examined in depth in the context of the child with ASD.

'The self-esteem of people who are always receiving help can never be high. Show us how we can help you too'.

(taken from an interview with Jim Sinclair, 2005)

Dependence upon others, for whatever reason, is a place that few of us would choose to be. Sometimes we work so closely to people 'who need our help' that we do not see that we are lowering their self-esteem. People who depend on us also need to feel cherished and know when we have valued their efforts.

Sometimes our focus on what needs to be taught takes our eye off the small gains being made. Even if it is sitting still for 30 seconds, the positive needs accentuating and articulating. If we do not feed back what we want them to do, e.g. 'Good sitting', they may not understand what is needed. If we always say 'Don't'/'Stop', we are not letting them know the expectations.

We can build on the self-esteem of children with ASD by starting with positive feedback. We can progress by providing a verbal commentary and an interpretation of what they are doing – 'Bahrat, that is good. You are getting out the crayons.' We need to be specific about what we value in their responses instead of correcting.

By taking time to be with the child, the message is that you value their company. Parallel play or engaging in their preferred pastime – provided it is legal/not offensive – may bring your presence to their attention, particularly if they are used to being solitary.

Activities contained in many PSHE resources (Salter and Twidle, 2005; Plimley and Cardwell, 1991; Moseley and Sonnet, 2003) can be used directly with more able children with ASD or adapted to more concrete tasks. A piece of card divided into two, or two plastic hoops where the child can sort things they like and dislike develops choice-making.

Skills audit

Make a record of things that they are good at. Many children with ASD focus on particular topics and build up an encyclopaedic knowledge of their 'special interest'. The term 'special interest' should not be a devalued, patronizing judgement. For us, 'Mastermind' conveys knowledge that is admired and applauded. Putting your music collection in order of the *date of birth* of the composer (Slater-Walker, 2004) is the type of interest a person with ASD may develop.

As a support worker you may need to give guidance and use ingenuity to help uncover their strengths. Sorting exercises, ways of rating their skills, day-to-day competencies that they (and you) may take for granted, need to be recorded for others to see and admire.

Understanding the mechanisms of school representation

The child with ASD may be good at determining positions of authority. You may find that your requests are being ignored until someone 'more powerful' arrives. If they only take direction from the highest authority, there needs to be a planned strategy to reinforce your position of responsibility. If the child can see that your opinion/information counts to the person in authority, then a strong message will be given.

Demonstrate a chain of command by giving each staff link their own discrete role. For example:

1. Meena has read two pages of her reading book to you
2. You tell the class teacher, who asks you to write this success in her home/school book
3. Parents thank you for letting them know
4. The class teacher puts Meena in for a special mention in the weekly 'show and tell' assembly

5. The head/deputy/head of year then rewards Meena in public and lets her choose a special gift from the box of rewards.

Many schools have a School's Council whereby elected pupil representatives can advocate and negotiate on behalf of their peers. School Councils are a common feature of secondary schools and their success at problem-solving, negotiating and decision-making is being replicated by primary schools and special schools. This mechanism may appeal to the child with ASD who has a strong sense of justice.

Encouraging the development of self-advocacy

The articulation of individual aspirations needs to begin early. Find opportunities for the child to exercise choice. For instance, eating and drinking: children with little expressive language can choose between apple/orange juice or raisins/crisps. Choices instil the concept that we have influence upon what is offered to us and what we take. There is a professional suspicion that offering choice might teach the concept of 'I can opt out of it', but choice is simply a means of finding a child's preferences in any situation.

What opportunities does the child with ASD that you know have for making choice within the school day? A child may be able to verbally express their wishes or use symbols/photos/objects of reference to choose:

- Toilet – yes or no
- Order of tasks – what's first?
- Breaktime – coat on/off
- Choice of partner in activities
- Drink or snack time
- Choice of colours in painting
- Choice of reward for completing tasks

Begin with simple choices where the alternatives are obvious. You choose the items and include one that is 99 per cent certain to be picked against one that would be a last resort.

Self-evaluation

Children with ASD often concentrate so hard and spend so much effort conforming at school that each thing that they produce is their very best effort. Suggesting improvement is tantamount to insult. However, there will be activities where they may rush through and not do their best. This is the time to introduce evaluation – how could this be improved? A look at products from classmates to point out the valued aspects or even tentatively offering criticism alongside understanding that 'You wanted this finished didn't you? It is not your best work'. If you have a good relationship with the child, they will probably take this from you.

The PSHE curriculum offered by your school should be encouraging children to make their wishes known, evaluate their strengths and focus on aspirations/targets. Circle time or other activities in the primary years help each child to provide an honest evaluation of their strengths and achievements. The child with ASD needs to be a part of these activities. The activities themselves will serve to boost the child's self-awareness and appraisal of their abilities.

CASE STUDY

At a specialist school for children with ASD in the Key Stage 2 class they end each day with a review of their achievements. Each child looks at the visual symbols that represent the passage of the school day and then picks out one activity where they did their best. This activity could be repeated at the end of each session but the children are assisted to remember what has happened during the day and if necessary digital photos or objects of reference are used to jog their recall. Using graphical representation or a picture that indicates one of their preferred interests (*Thomas the Tank* or *Harry Potter* could be used) they identify the activity that they worked well in and then they put their picture next to it. This serves the purpose of being a structured basic opportunity to reflect on what they have done and assess their positive input.

(From an idea by Prior's Court School, Newbury)

REFLECTIVE OASIS

What could be used to give the child/ren that you know the opportunity to reflect on the effort they have made in a lesson?

How could you introduce simple-choice making into the child's daily activities?

How can these opportunities to assess their strengths and aspirations be made in an accessible way?

One of the obvious ways in which the views of the child can be sought is by being a part of the SEN review process. The Individual Education Plan is a step along the way to the Annual review. Shore (2004), a person with ASD, believes that the child with ASD can be encouraged to have a voice in setting IEP targets. He says:

> One of the prerequisites for success in this critical area is to establish a sense of self-determination within the child: that is an understanding of one's preferences in the context of one's strengths and challenges. One way to instil a sense of self-determination is to help the child make a list of her likes and dislikes, while at the same time encouraging her to examine how closely her preferences line up with her strong points. (p24)

For the child who has no concept of what they are good at, give fulsome acknowledgement: 'You know where everything goes, help me find ...' This then can become a script that is repeated until the child starts saying it too: 'I can find anything in this room.' These will be the building blocks of their involvement in the IEP process. For some the attendance at an IEP meeting may be the limit of their involvement (Shore, 2004), but for others, able to articulate their strengths and targets, a bigger part can be played.

The Nottinghamshire Inclusion Support Service use a proforma printed passport as a primary–secondary school transition aid that:

- contains a written 'snapshot' of who the child is
- what their strengths and achievements are
- how they would like to be approached
- how to calm them down when stressed
- how they display their emotions, especially happiness

The child completes the passport profile and parents' views are added. Continuity of information and identification of positive attributes are held by both settings and have other applications (Cook and Stowe, 2003).

Dealing with bullies

Your role as a support worker will give you insight into how your establishment works for you, as an employee and the person you are supporting. The condition of ASD has been described as a 'conundrum' and we are the detectives who unravel the mystery of why Tommy behaved like that. We make ASD our 'special interest' because their actions and words can develop into a fascination for us.

The downside of working in any large establishment is the possible existence of bullying. People with ASD often cannot recognize the social signals that bullying is taking place. Luke Jackson, a young man with Asperger Syndrome, sets out the parameters for people with ASD, when he describes bullying:

Physical bullying includes *any* form of unwanted touching at all:

- Kicking, hitting, shoving.
- Pushing out of the line (i.e. the dinner queue) in order to get me into trouble.
- Pushing in front of me in queues so that I am always left at the back.
- Sticking their foot out and tripping me up ...
- Knocking the dinner tray out of my hand.
- Kicking and prodding through the back of the chair.
- Pulling an odd strand of hair or poking me ...
- Doors being slammed in my face.

Other forms of bullying

- Rulers, pencils and other equipment taken ...
- School books scribbled and drawn on ...
- Ink squirted at me, covering my clothes.
- Packed lunch taken and squashed onto the floor.
- Name calling and teasing ...
- Being deliberately ignored ... when I am speaking whilst everyone laughs about it.
- Being left till the end when teams are being picked ...
- Ridiculed for not being good at team sports. I am used to the familiar groan of 'Aw, Sir, do we have to have him?'

(Jackson, 2002, pp139–40)

If you witness bullying, you may have to act immediately or report it to someone who can deal with it. You may even feel like the victim, if the taunts and teasing happen while you are there. It is not a weakness to admit that it is happening and your presence has not stopped it. Try to see this as an opportunity to act decisively and effectively.

Unfortunately there are still work cultures that belittle sensitive and caring staff members. Jackson fears the retribution of bullying teachers:

Teachers can bully too. I hope that I do not get into trouble for writing this. I am sure that lots of teachers are either keen to help those of us who are a bit different, or at the very least are willing to just let us get on with life without hassling us. I have to say though that there are some teachers who seem to be bigger bullies than the kids in the school.

The first thing to do if a teacher is picking on you or upsetting you is to tell them very clearly that they are upsetting you. If they ignore you, then you must go and tell the head of your year or the headteacher or even another teacher who you do trust.

(Jackson, 2002, pp142–3)

You may have to advocate on behalf of the pupil directly with school colleagues or by talking to the parent/carer about bullying. Jackson suggests that if you are seeking information, be specific. Not 'Are you being bullied?', but 'Has someone hurt/kicked/punched you?' He also says it is insensitive to talk about incidents and maltreatment in front of the child to anybody. This has the effect of making them feel further isolated and can also provoke further bullying. As a support worker it is vital to ensure that this unhappy experience does not blight the rest of their education.

Points to remember

- The value of a skills audit
- The importance of developing self-esteem
- Create opportunities to foster independence and for pupil participation
- Develop protocols to protect pupils with ASD from bullying

Working with colleagues

The role of the support worker and their position within a school's structure is highlighted in this chapter. Areas of working practices that are liable to cause the support worker stress are examined in more depth with some practical suggestions on how to avoid stress and discord in the working day.

The work of the effective support worker cannot exist in isolation. To work to your maximum potential you will need close contact with and effective strategies for the pupil/s you support and you will need to relate to others whose roles overlap your own.

Think of the number of people you come across in a typical school day. There is a whole host of other adults who are also involved in the nature of your work.

CASE STUDY

Steve worked in a secondary special school. His role was to support a young man with ASD and SLD. When Steve first started in his job, he listed how many people he met in a day and their names.

8.45   KS3 briefing – Shirley, Ricky, Ann, Maggie, Sheenaz and Royston

9.05   Buses arrive – Win – bus guide and Mervyn, driver

9.15   Registration – Barbara and Linda – secretaries

9.30   Assembly – 20 people and Head, Ms Wilson

(Continued)

9.45	SALT – Marjorie arrives
9.50–12.20	Teaching and break time
12.20–1.10	Lunch time. Phone call with Mrs B, mother of person Steve works with
1.10	Breaktime – 8 supervisors
1.45	Swimming with Caroline – swimming teacher
2.30	Occupational therapist – Aziz arrives
3.20	Bus time – Win and Mervyn and 10 other bus guides and drivers

Total of people Steve encounters in a school day = 47

REFLECTIVE OASIS

How many other adults do you come across in a school day?

Is it more or fewer than Steve?

Can you name all of the other adults?

How do their roles impinge upon your own?

Not everyone that you come into contact with has an influence upon your work, although there are some key people who play a significant role:

- Other support workers in your area/class
- Teachers whom you have daily contact with
- Medical/ancillary personnel associated with your child with ASD
- The child's parents/carers
- Members of the school's Senior Management Team (SMT) making staff deployment decisions
- Anyone who line-manages you.

A breakdown in communication, supervision of your work and how valued you feel could result in you becoming disaffected. Relationships with key people are a necessity to do the best job you can, and to have job satisfaction.

Tyrer, Gunn, Lee, Parker, Pittman and Townsend (2004) surveyed common stressors of the support worker. Three of the nine categories – lack of communication; time together planning; short notice of teacher expectation and support worker's role, were given as popular sources of stress. Tyrer *et al*. (2004) say that for any teacher/supporter relationship to work, there need to be good levels of understanding, compromise and empathy. Balshaw (1999, cited in Tyrer *et al.*, 2004) gives six principles to be observed so that support workers feel part of a collaborative working team:

- Clearly defined roles and responsibilities
- Good levels of communication
- Consistency of approach
- A team that works together
- Good standard of personal and professional skills
- Attending to staff development needs.

If you are experiencing a breakdown in any aspect of your working relationships then rating these areas personally may help you to pinpoint the specific area that needs more attention.

The child with ASD needs a staff group who can work collaboratively and well together. So do all children receiving this type of support but the area that is crucial for the child with ASD is continuity among the people involved in their lives. Their acquisition of skills and knowledge can depend on incidental features that we may not notice. The extra dimension of sensory differences can only impact on this further. Skills and knowledge learned in one setting/with one person are not automatically generalized to other settings/people. Your role is critical:

- to communicate their experiences and responses
- to interpret events and requests for them
- to transmit ways in which their learning experiences can be enhanced.

While your relationship with the teacher is key to how the child experiences school, your collaboration with:

- ancillary staff
- supervisory staff
- transport guides and drivers
- administrative staff
- therapists
- parents and family
- Senior Management Team

may mean the difference between the child having a positive or negative day.

My role/their role

The professionalization of an historically poorly paid workforce, coupled with some clear expectations, is long overdue. You may also be bringing your own specialism/skills into the role as well as personal competencies from outside of working time. A supportive school will identify and nurture your 'value added' talents. If your school does not conduct a skills audit of new recruits, then you need to put your case forward.

Twenty special school teachers at the Autism Cymru Special School Forum (2005) listed the tasks that they asked their support workers to undertake:

- Support the teacher and pupils, taking direction from their line manager
- Daily care of pupil/s
- Assist with resources in lesson preparation
- Take responsibility for display boards and craft activities
- Be an effective team member and provide regular feedback
- Attend relevant training sessions
- Lesson support – 1:1 or small group and also support integration exercises
- Be positive and demonstrate initiative
- The extension of a teacher's role
- Home tuition for pupils who cannot come into school
- Support the teacher with the implementation of IEPs within the classroom

CASE STUDY

Two special school support workers wrote down the different ways in which they fulfilled their role.

- We provide a friendly, safe and cheerful environment
- We give consistency and continuity to promote social and emotional development
- We involve children in play, develop social skills, build trust and boost confidence
- We prompt answers by asking searching questions
- We support children to work at their own pace and to avoid distractions
- We record the understanding of the child
- We join in with the pupils
- We model responses
- We record what the pupils do

(With thanks to Kelly and Lisa at Heol Goffa Special School, Carmarthenshire)

The Forum teachers identified ways to increase their expectations of support workers who have further qualifications, like an NVQ 3:

- To support teaching and learning at all levels
- To aid inclusion
- To work on specialist programmes
- To develop their own specialism, e.g. IT, behaviour, therapy assistance, etc.

The role of Higher Level Teaching Assistant has its own set of requirements and responsibilities. A section of the Teacher Training Agency standards focuses on how support workers are expected to interact and work collaboratively with colleagues:

1.4 They work collaboratively with colleagues and carry out their roles effectively, knowing when to seek help and advice.

1.5 They are able to liaise sensitively and effectively with parents and carers, recognizing their roles in pupils' learning

1.6 They are able to improve their own practice, including through observation, evaluation and discussion with colleagues.

3.1.1 They contribute effectively to teachers' planning and preparation of lessons

3.1.2 Working within a framework set by the teacher, they plan their role in lessons including how they will provide feedback to pupils and colleagues on pupils' learning and behaviour.

3.2.3 They monitor pupils' participation and progress, providing feedback to teachers and giving constructive support to pupils as they learn.

3.3.5 They are able, where relevant, to guide the work of other adults supporting teaching and learning in the classroom'.

(TTA Standards, taken from Tyrer *et al.*, 2004)

You may wish to reflect on how closely you match these expectations of professional collaboration.

Offering support and getting support for yourself

The final standard is about helping, advising and supporting others to fulfil their roles effectively. The coordination of support workers is managed by the individual teacher. The way in which you work, collaborate and communicate will depend on the style and personality of the worker. Support workers as a collective team need to have a forum in which they can safely and constructively voice their achievements, concerns and issues. One way of doing this is suggested in the next chapter. Your school may also organize class/base/departmental meetings that you are expected to attend and contribute to. While this is an effective mechanism for dealing with class teaching and learning, it may not be where you can air other concerns.

You are going to be aware of other support colleagues who may be having a difficult time. If you notice that a new member of staff is feeling isolated in their work, offer advice or just listen to their problems. Support workers tend to come from a wide cross-section of ages and backgrounds and more men are joining their ranks. Encouraging open and honest communication, a degree of loyalty is the proactive way to forge empathetic relationships. Avoid cliques because these divide staffs and lead to unhappy and unproductive working situations. Finally, when looking for more support, turn to the person who line-manages you. This could be your teacher or another member of staff. Try to meet regularly with that person to discuss general issues, e.g. job satisfaction and overall professional development. This need not be a daily or weekly appointment but 30 minutes every month may make a difference to how you view your work contribution and what you can offer.

Points to remember

- Collaborate and communicate at a number of levels
- Define roles and responsibilities to avoid misunderstandings

Being assertive and having your say

Following on from the previous chapter the skills and qualities needed for successful support work are examined in depth. Ways of identifying your own strengths and promoting your contribution to and participation in school life are looked at.

A monthly support worker meeting – during assembly time/lunch time or, providing everyone agrees, a meeting after school – is a way in which support workers can feel as if they are listened to and valued.

CASE STUDY

On the first Wednesday of each month, the deputy of a primary school held a 45-minute support staff meeting. This happened during singing practice. The deputy made it clear that support workers were not to be called upon, as this was their time.

Each week prior to the meeting, the deputy circulated an agenda, inviting points to be discussed at the meeting. Though support assistants did not always contribute, it was a way of showing their views were valued.

The deputy took the meeting minutes and made a copy for each support worker by the end of the day of the meeting.

The meetings had items of school information – arrangements for trips/sports days etc. It looked at rotas, job parity, responsibilities.

(Continued)

Details for further professional development were shared. The support workers brought other topics of interest and could address personal/professional problems.

The effectiveness of the meetings was illustrated by organized termly evenings out – meals, bowling, cinema, badminton, etc. The group had formed a cohesion and enjoyment in each other's company that was extended outside school.

REFLECTIVE OASIS

Does your school enable support workers to meet together?

Is this a support mechanism that is/could be valued?

What types of issues are/could be raised at support meetings?

The meetings are a safe and constructive means to air your differences. The actual meeting structure avoids the temptation for issues to get out of hand. Negativity will not be encouraged if it is handled by a firm chair person. Being assertive is something that needs to be practised and developed over time.

Scenario

Ayesha, a support worker, is upset that her colleagues get a longer break than her because of the needs of the child with ASD she is supporting. Sympathetic but smug noises have been made – 'It's a shame for you to be out there, while we're still drinking our coffee …'

Ayesha wants to do something about it and she has three choices.

Passive

She accepts that she will not be able to change anything. Her colleagues see her as a victim for not raising it with her line manager.

Aggressive

She demands to see the line manager and launches into a tirade about fairness and feeling stressed. Her colleagues see her as stroppy.

Assertive

She meets with her line manager and tells him in a firm, measured way that she is spending an extra 15 minutes working each day, compared to her colleagues. She invites her line manager to problem-solve with her. The solution is that she has an extra break during the IT session when her pupil can be unsupported. Her colleagues see she has got a fair deal.

Being assertive is waiting for your moment and putting your thoughts across in the most constructive manner. Wait for the emotion to die down before you act and you can feel more certain that you are not going to shout, whine or cry. Practise in a mirror or with a trusted friend. To be assertive and deal with a problem, you need to:

- deal with the facts only
- use a measured tone and neutral language
- not engage in gossip or speculation
- say how the event/person makes you feel
- ask the listener to help you solve the problem/reframe your experience
- look your listener in the eye so they can appreciate how serious this is for you.

Assertiveness is not just about problem-solving. It can be 'a way of life' to enable everyone to have their say and reach acceptable decisions. It is about everyone getting to air their views and reach a compromise or take a vote on the outcome.

Identifying your personal strengths and weaknesses

You bring a wealth of experiences and abilities to your role. These will not just be related to the role you have been recruited for, although they will have played a significant part in the application and interview process. Most application forms have a section for you to list your interests and hobbies. People who shortlist applications for interview will pay more attention to those applicants who have put something extra in that box. Peeters and Jordan (1999) say it is not sufficient to be interested in supporting children with ASD – talented and memorable people in this work often have something extra to give.

Our pastimes can become more significant in our work with children with ASD. Our empathy and ability to remember what it was like to be a child can be a tool in tailoring our responses to the children we work with. Children with ASD will pay attention to people who engage in the same interests as themselves. They will notice someone who will willingly join in with their games. Remember, they are usually told not to do those things.

You may find that many people who work with people with ASD will have ideas of how to change the person. What is rarer is someone who says 'I accept the child as they are … I am going to support their growth and development'. Acceptance is what you can give to the person with ASD at the start of your relationship with them. This foundation can then take direction and flourish from the experiences you share together.

People with ASD seem to have an uncanny knack of spotting 'frauds' in the people they know. They are able to sense who is there for them and who is not. They are good at knowing who they frighten. If you are true to yourself and project a calm and confident image, the person with ASD will come to understand and respect that. If you can offer them your own strengths and interests to enhance their experiences then they will learn from your enthusiasm and motivation.

It is also important to know when you are out of your depth. The ability to admit to your own faults and weaknesses is part of self-awareness. We each have a limit to what we can tolerate. Sometimes the role of supporting a person with ASD tests us to our limits.

CASE STUDY

Delroy was a keen body builder who supported Marvin, a young man with ASD. Marvin knew that Delroy would not tolerate the more difficult aspects of his behaviour – punching, kicking. Delroy and Marvin had a mutual respect for each other and this was enhanced by Delroy jogging round the track with Marvin when he became agitated.

Delroy attended his local church where he sang in the choir. Marvin had perfect singing pitch so they were able to enjoy singing as a

(Continued)

(Continued)

release of tension. What Delroy could not accept though, was Marvin's use of swear words when he got upset. Delroy took Marvin's swearing as an attack on his beliefs and he struggled to work with Marvin when this happened.

Delroy started to think he may have to give up his job, because it was getting him down. However, after a discussion, the SENCo had some new ideas on how Delroy could manage this behaviour by using a social story (Gray, 2000) to help Marvin find other ways of expressing his discontent.

Delroy worked with Marvin and his social story to reinforce the idea that he should ask for help. Then he could leave the situation to run one lap of the track to defuse the tension, before returning to complete his task with Delroy's consistent and dependable help.

Playing a role in planning and practice

Teaching staff and headteachers have been encouraged by government initiatives and the backing of their unions to reassess what they feel is vital to the role of teacher in the classroom. Hall (2005, cited in Campbell and Fairburn, 2005) says that for optimum use of the support worker, the teacher needs to 'share his/her thoughts about how to teach the group'. This means the support worker being involved in lessons and decisions on how to support the individual/group. Hall (2005) goes on to cite the DfES (2000):

> all the evidence shows that the team of teacher and TA works at its highest level when the TA is informed by the teacher of the plans and intentions for the lesson and is consulted over its execution.

This will work if the teacher, or the school as a whole, can see the value and have a clear purpose for its use of support workers. The benefits of such collaboration will be numerous – from having a less stressed colleague (teacher) to having a confident 'second in command' (support worker).

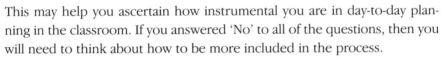

REFLECTIVE OASIS

Think of a recent lesson:

Did the teacher communicate what the lesson entailed?

Did you have planning input?

Did having advance knowledge of the lesson help you to support the pupil?

Tailor their learning – via differentiation or how the task was presented?

Enhance the outcome of the lesson?

Make you feel your contribution was welcome?

This may help you ascertain how instrumental you are in day-to-day planning in the classroom. If you answered 'No' to all of the questions, then you will need to think about how to be more included in the process.

Recent publications (Tyrer *et al.,* 2004; Campbell and Fairburn, 2005) highlight the crucial importance of the support worker in the classroom. A mini-consensus at the Autism Cymru Special School Forum (2005) looked at the range of roles their support workers undertake:

- Part of regular staff meetings for discussion/planning
- Involvement in recording (verbal and written) observation of IEPs
- Preparing adequate resources relevant to pupil needs
- Having an annual staff appraisal

How to get your message across

The previous scenario of Ayesha is a study of how to react to perceived injustices. You may want to 'save face' and preserve your dignity if you are going to broach issues that are unresolved. Assertiveness is the key, with tenacity and the ability to work out your 'strategy'. Consider what you need to say and take time (and advice) to work out how you are going to say it.

When dealing with serious situations that are causing you stress or are making you think about leaving your job, then you may consider these 'added' strategies:

- Ask the listener for their interpretation
- Repeat how you are feeling
- Insist that you want to resolve the situation
- Mention that the situation is becoming serious for you
- Invite a move towards a solution or compromise

Keep your focus sharp and do not let dialogue deteriorate into a 'he said/she said' situation. Almost certainly, these approaches will work with the colleague who can resolve it for you.

Finally, if it fails to produce the outcome you would like, follow these options:

- The 'broken record' – repeat the same information
- Go to the next person above the one you have already approached
- You may need to go to the top regarding deliberate exclusive practices, poor staff attitude, inappropriate teaching or management of support staff.

Any suspicion of child abuse needs to proceed directly to the named child protection coordinator in the school.

 Points to remember

- Create support networks
- Be assertive and promote your own strengths
- Contribute to planning and practice

10

Managing expectations

The pressures of working in a school environment where the expectations of others are critical and the support worker has a range of roles to deliver are discussed in this chapter. Positive ways of managing expectations are illustrated to help the support worker achieve a realistic perspective.

The role of the support worker has traditionally existed within special schools. In the early 1970s after the legislation that gave every child with a disability a right to education (DES Circular 12/70), special schools employed local people, usually women, as welfare assistants. Sometimes you still hear support workers being called a 'welfare'. Their role was largely the toileting and feeding needs of the pupils. Sometimes they worked in the classroom, under the direction of the class teacher. Enlightened establishments from the 1980s onwards have enhanced and empowered support workers to take a leading role within the classroom. The current view of support workers is as a crucial help to teachers and the whole school.

The pay and conditions of support roles have traditionally been undervalued and viewed as term-time jobs for women with children of school age. Some local authority agreements have ensured that support work appeals only to those with an existing primary household income, the pay structure for this work has been so poor. More enlightened schools and LEA officers have sought to retain their hard-working staff during holiday periods and have structured their conditions to attain this. Government initiatives in England (Education Act 2002, DfES, 2003) and Wales (National Assembly for Wales,

2004) have contributed to a more informed, dedicated workforce – those who wish to can be paid to work while they train to be a teacher (TTA, 2005).

Since the move towards inclusion in mainstream schools, there are more advertised posts for support workers. The inclusion of pupils with physical or sensory disabilities in mainstream schools usually comes with a contract of support hours. While support workers are recognized as valuable in assisting the child with a physical disability with their care needs, their role in the classroom is not always appreciated. Many mainstream teachers have been used to being in charge of their own domain and are not used sharing their space. In primary schools that time has now passed and teachers benefit from skilled support. In secondary schools, it is still a new phenomenon but the transition time will pass. The role that support workers assume can vary from establishment to establishment. Table 10.1 lists some of their potential duties.

Table 10.1   Potential support worker duties

• Organizer	• Field trip organizer
• Administrator	• Male/female member of staff for public toilets
• First-aider	
• Display coordinator	• Minibus driver
• 1:1 supporter	• Photocopier
• Small group work support	• Class records compiler
• Table-manners enforcer	• Resource organizer
• Feeder of those who require help	• Bottom-wiper
• Lesson planner	• Toilet trainer
• Evaluator	• Laundress
• Observer	• Clothes repairer
• Resource maker	• Technician
• Resource finder	• Troubleshooter
• Parent communicator	• Assembly presence
	• Health and safety officer

Tick off how many you have been asked to do within one day. One of the positive things about the work is that there's rarely any time to feel bored! A teacher who uses their support staff well will know how valuable it is to have them there. A good support worker can be as effective as any teacher, so long as they are respected, appreciated and not exploited.

Other colleagues might have their own expectations. You are proably not the only support worker. Good communication needs to exist between all adults within school. Effective deployment of staff does not mean that you have to be with one pupil all day, every day. Even though your support contract may stipulate hours to support John Smith, a creative teacher will use you in many other ways. It is counterproductive to use support staff in the 'velcroed' position of never leaving the same child's side for the whole school day. It is not a good idea for the child to see you as their possession or not to share you with other pupils. If the child with ASD is particularly challenging, you may also reach a point of burnout with them. Support staff with sole responsibility for one child can be too protective of the child and effectively disable them from trying out new experiences. You may be supporting a child for whom you have no patience and/or they have no tolerance for you. Far better, then, to share out support of pupils, to allow them to tolerate more people in that role.

It may be a productive task for you do a SWOT (Strengths Weaknesses, Opportunities, Threats) analysis to check on how well you feel used and appreciated within your role. Objective analysis can flag up some unmet needs or staff undercurrents that you had not been aware of Table 10.2 is a specimen SWOT analysis of Jane B, a support worker in a primary school.

Table 10.2 Jane's SWOT analysis

Strengths	Weaknesses
• Job is near to home • I can get in early every day • I like working with Year 4 • I have a variety of roles • I am good at display work • I get on well with Mrs W (classteacher)	• I have to stay late on Monday • I do not always have a lunch break • Matthew P does not like working with me • I will be working with Y6 next year • I would prefer to do display stuff during assembly time
Opportunities	**Threats**
• I can attend training on ASD next term • Mrs P would like me to visit Matthew at home • Year 6 do wonderful interactive displays • Kelly (support worker) will help out with Matthew P • I could ask to stay late another night • I could alternate with Kelly at lunch time	• Mrs W refuses to let me miss assemblies • Class 6 will not like me • My role becomes smaller • Kelly will not help me out • Someone else goes on the training

You can see at a glance from Jane's SWOT analysis that she has obvious skills and aptitudes, currently well used in Year 4. Her worries lie within the uncertain future in Year 6 and whether her skills will be recognized there. She also feels that her relationship with one of the pupils she supports (Matthew P) may not be successful. However, his mother values her help and has invited her to visit them at home. She is currently under pressure to work through her lunch hours and attend the Monday night meeting. By organizing her thoughts and looking at things objectively, she gives everything another perspective.

Probably the hardest box to fill in in a SWOT analysis is your strengths, as we find it hard to admit to having them! Jane has managed to do that and is also raising issues and solutions via this mechanism. She now has a framework for negotiation with current colleagues and to flag up in her future Year 6 role.

SWOT analysis helps you to get everything down on paper and deal with issues proactively. If Jane had not committed her innermost concerns to paper she may have continued to brood upon them, or let the uncertainties assume an exaggerated importance.

REFLECTIVE OASIS

Use the headings for the SWOT analysis

- Strengths
- Weaknesses
- Opportunities
- Threats

and compile one for you in your present role.

Points to remember

- Your professional and personal development needs to be monitored and evaluated regularly if you are to remain content in your work
- Conduct a SWOT analysis before a staff appraisal

11

Developing professional relationships

Ways of managing your workload and having a professional contribution to make in your school are looked at in this chapter. This is expanded into relationships with parents and carers, as support workers play a key role in keeping lines of communication open.

Sometimes colleagues can misunderstand the characteristics of the child with ASD and you hold a privileged position in your relationship with the child. You could be the role model for good practice for the pupil you support. In a supportive and positive working environment you will be given credit for your ASD-friendly practice. This, however, may single you out and serve to isolate you from your other colleagues. It is important to deal with these undercurrents in a professional manner.

To be a professional in school is to be aware of all aspects of the job and to fulfil those roles in a competent and efficient manner. You can do a self-audit of your competency/efficiency by checking your job description and making sure that you fulfil each aspect. Then you need to consider the wider role you play and the other skills and knowledge you bring to the post. You might also think about your relationship with the child/ren you support and whether this is having benefits for them.

Unprofessional behaviours are often not noticed by the perpetrator and may even be a part of their personality. Look at this list of behaviours that children said they did not appreciate in a support worker (Tyrer *et al.*, 2004):

- Patronizing
- Doing things that they did not need to
- Being controlling and frightening off children who would be friends

- Always negative
- Not able to help them with their work (did not understand it)
- Under-protective
- Over-protective
- Not wishing to get to know the child

Add to this list the features of an unprofessional member of staff:

- Poor time-keeper
- Gossips behind back of others
- Unreliable
- Poor standard of work
- Does not care
- Undermines colleagues
- Has no professional distance from child/ren
- Poor role model
- Unwilling to do anything extra

By reframing these negatives into their opposites (e.g. unreliable into reliable) we can identify positive professional strengths. If you can identify why you are not getting on with a colleague, you are part-way towards finding a solution. Often those who do not show professionalism at work are lacking in a role model. They may need clearer and repeated guidelines. Do not dismiss a colleague because they are not currently engaging in your professional standards. Offer to be a 'buddy'/mentor to them so that they can learn from you. Where the unprofessional person is senior to you, you need to pass on your perceptions to them (assertiveness) if it is impacting upon you. Or pass it onto their line manager, if it is disadvantaging the child/ren you support.

> **CASE STUDY**
>
> Parmajit had always given her best support to a pupil with Asperger syndrome from when he joined in Year 7. That pupil had now left and gone onto college. During her five years at the school, Parmajit had taken an interest in Asperger Syndrome and read the literature that the SENCo had given her. She had also attended two twilight sessions on awareness raising.
>
> She was asked to support a new pupil with Asperger Syndrome, Jason. He needed full-time support and Parmajit only worked 15 hours per week. Shereen, who Parmajit knew from her community, was appointed as a job-share. Shereen was a younger member of staff

(Continued)

who had her own social agenda. Shereen was punctual and spent time 'handing over' to Parmajit but it was clear that Shereen would not give any extra time. After a couple of months in her job, Shereen started having short periods of sickness.

Jason started to ask Parmajit why she had to leave everyday, because he 'did not like that other girl'. She was concerned when she heard that Jason had started to be disruptive when she was not there.

Parmajit asked Shereen about her job commitment and fed back what Jason had said. Shereen was not surprised; Jason had often said it to her. She was not enjoying working with such an ungrateful child.

Parmajit started talking to Shereen about the positives of working with Jason and the progress he was making. She asked Shereen what she knew about Asperger. Shereen admitted she knew very little, but added there was something fascinating about Jason. Parmajit offered to help Shereen understand Asperger. She lent her books/resources and they also both attended training in Asperger Syndrome on a teacher training day. Parmajit suggested that they both give up an hour a week voluntarily to co-work with Jason so that Parmajit's skills could be passed onto Shereen.

The ideas that Parmajit shared enabled them to increase the consistency and continuity of approach to Jason and he really appreciated having the security of two predictable adults.

REFLECTIVE OASIS

Can you offer to share your professionalism and commitment with a colleague?

What skills and knowledge do you have that could benefit their work?

How do you make the first move?

Effective collaboration with colleagues

Collaboration is another level up from 'working together'. It entails a system for working, communicating and achieving the best possible outcomes for the child. It implies a coordination of input, an identification of targets and a prescribed role to play. The efficacy of collaboration has a measurable end product, whether that is through an informal evaluation, an appraisal or more formal testing measures. The SENCo may be the person coordinating collaborative work. The key outcomes to this are support workers who:

- fully understand their role and the valuable contribution they make to teaching and learning in the school,
- work collaboratively with the SENCo, teaching staff and staff from external agencies,
- develop their skills to become more knowledgeable of ways in which pupils can be supported, helping them to maximize their levels of achievement and independence

Effective collaboration is focused and specific. It involves key professionals in the education of the child with ASD spending time together planning and evaluating the processes of teaching and learning. Autism Cymru Special School Forum (2005) developed a list of ideas for improving collaborative practices in school:

- Involvement in the planning process at multidisciplinary level
- Observing/recording for other professionals, e.g. SALT, physiotherapist, etc.
- Experienced staff supporting new members
- Sharing information, e.g. medical, behaviour to class teacher

Quite often different people will contribute very different things, but that is part of the process. By collaborating with people in a similar role you will gain valuable insights into the understanding of how different people work. Spending time on observational tasks, not just of the child/ren but of other professionals, can enable a clearer understanding of how roles overlap and interact. Your school may also have inclusion links with other schools and the opportunity to go and work in a mainstream or a special school can bring rewards in terms of collaborative practices.

Sharing ideas with parents and colleagues

Sharing ideas and practices with colleagues has been included in this book. You will come across those members of staff who are interested in ASD. The 'drip-drip' approach will help you to counteract the negative remarks of others. Other ways of sharing ideas with colleagues are more strategic and may include your contribution to the drafting of the mission statement, the revision of the school's prospectus, the links with neighbouring schools or the governing body. These kinds of roles will serve to heighten and enhance the sharing of good ASD practice.

The school's relationships with parents are always going to be crucial, even more so when their child has ASD. The experiences of families and parents of children with ASD are outlined in another book (Attfield and Morgan, 2006) in this series. Many parents and carers feel that they have had to battle from the moment they recognized a difference in their child. They bring those combative strategies to school, because they think that is the only way to achieve things for their child. We can regard the tenacity of the parents of some children with ASD as troublesome.

It cannot be stressed too strongly that the parents are the experts in their child. They have known him/her the longest and share a total view of their every day. They are the people who have sought an answer to the differences in their child's development and they have received the diagnosis and, very often, gone away to find out more. You may have a view that they are over-protective, under-protective, too fussy, not fussy enough. That is your view. You cannot possibly appreciate the ways in which they have had to adapt to a child with ASD. Autism Cymru Primary School Forum (2005) listed some of the ways in which parents can act to frustrate pathways towards inclusion:

- Levels of anxiety about the mainstream school
- Attitudes towards LEA and their choice of school
- Lack of awareness of what inclusion will entail

They conclude that it is important that schools and school staff do try to understand where parents are coming from. You need to listen to what they are saying.

Kluth (2003) believes that school staff can get to understand family experiences by finding out more about the family unit, including siblings, grandparents, aunts/uncles. Recognize that the care and understanding of the child is part of the wider family role. Try to achieve common ground in aims and aspirations for their child and understand the family's view on ASD and disability. By talking, listening to and respecting their experiences, we can reframe our view of their attitudes. This cannot just happen at the annual parents' evening; the content may be too emotional and the scene too public. Taking time and providing the right circumstances for a supportive and sharing relationship to grow will be a priority.

The support worker is often a key person in maintaining relationships with home. They are often the person who fills in the home–school book or makes the regular phone call home. This should be viewed as a valued activity which will enhance the school experiences of the child. Kluth (2003) lists a range of ways that the whole school can seek to support the parent/carer of a child with ASD:

- A welcoming school – the whole ethos supports and accepts the contribution of parents. Hold coffee mornings or activity groups for parents to join in.
- Believe all children are important – parents know that their child is valued because staff have taken time to get to know them. Focus on the child's strengths and how they can achieve a valued classroom/school role.
- Communication is open, constant and productive – parents are not made to feel as if it is inconvenient or inappropriate. Involve parents and families in problem-solving the latest issues.
- Keep communication channels open by mobile phone texting, mobile phone pictures, emails, an attachment of the child's work or a photo of what they are doing, video/audio tapes as well as phone calls and written messages.
- Be keen to learn from the family – use their expertise. Invite parents to talk about ASD and their child in particular to an interest group/INSET session.
- Clear structures for information and sharing of knowledge – having other means of global communication like a class or school newsletter, invitation to social events, the prospectus, IEP meetings and parents' evenings.

The support worker can play an integral part in nurturing home–school links. They may also be the person who can be sensitive towards parents' needs and who can tailor contact and information sharing at difficult times.

CASE STUDY

Mr and Mrs Keow knew that their daughter Sianting was developing differently when she was 4 months old. After 3 years, they saw a specialist who diagnosed ASD. Sianting attended a small local primary school. The staff met with Mrs Keow every day and discussed Sianting. When Sianting reached the age of 8, the staff felt that she would benefit from a special school placement.

She travelled 10 miles to her special school. The support worker wrote home every day and often appended pieces of work or digital photos of Sianting's activities. Mrs Keow offered to help the school with their Christmas productions. She regularly came to help out with resources in class. Sometimes she brought Sianting's granny as they were both good at drawing and sewing.

The involvement of the family in the activity of the school continued until Sianting left to go onto college.

The Keow family retained a strong link to the school and now sponsors an Annual Citizenship Award for children at the school.

REFLECTIVE OASIS

Is your school doing all it can to encourage the support of parents?

Are there ways that parents can contribute their experiences to a shared understanding of the child with ASD?

Are wider family members involved in the school's activities?

Points to remember

- The importance of raising staff awareness of ASD at every opportunity
- Make sure colleagues fully understand your role and value your expertise
- Give parents time and understanding to develop a vital working relationship

12

What is possible in your role

Finally in this chapter we look at what the support worker can do to be an effective member of staff. The positive qualities of effective supporters of people with ASD are looked at as well as how to work with your other commitments and how to maximise your potential for a satisfying working life.

The authors recognize that support workers cannot effect change alone. Most support workers enjoy their work, and its variety often reinforces their working relationship with the children. Many things are possible provided we have the time, the motivation and the valuing feedback from our colleagues.

Peeters and Jordan (1999) believe that 'extraordinary people require extraordinary professionals' in the field of autism. They say that there can be an element of feeling de-skilled, when every day presents new challenges and confusing reactions. These feelings do not necessarily go away because you have worked with children with ASD before. Each child will have a unique blend of characteristics, personality, character and family traits that make us ponder. Peeters and Jordan (1999) have outlined 12 potential qualities which will enable us to become effective practitioners in the field of ASD. These are condensed into eight attributes below:

1 Be attracted by differences

Our curiosity will make us want to find out more about the condition of ASD and do the best that we can. We do not shy away from situations that challenge the way in which we work.

2 Have a vivid imagination

Individuals with ASD are often lacking in their ability to 'put themselves in the shoes of other people', described as a lack of empathy. Those who enjoy their work with children with ASD often have empathy and imagination in abundance and can gauge where they are coming from.

3 Be able to get by without the usual thank-yous

Sometimes the work you do is invisible or hard to quantify. People with ASD may not be able 'see' the high support you are giving. Your inbuilt interest in what you are doing and your ability to see progress in the smallest advance is very rewarding.

4 Be willing to adapt your style of communication and social interaction

We learn by trial and error how to phrase, request and convey information. A successful support worker will be willing to learn new and different ways of communicating and working with the child with ASD.

5 Always thirst for more knowledge

We will probably never know 'enough' about ASD and we need to leave ourselves open to learning continuously throughout our careers. We must not be afraid to put new ideas and strategies into action, providing there is respect for the dignity of the child and ethical considerations are not compromised.

6 Accept that each bit of progress will bring a new puzzle

Peeters and Jordan (1999) say

> Once you start, you know that the 'detective' work is never over. Nor is there some 'expert' somewhere who knows all the answers and never makes mistakes. Working with autism means a commitment to sticking with it, recognizing one's mistakes and accepting that there may be times, or aspects of energy, empathy and a commitment to ultimate success. (p88)

7 Be prepared to work as a team

One of the keys to effective work with people with ASD is consistency and continuity. By having a partnership with parents, skills and knowledge can be applied and practised. Work closely with parents and keep open communication to ensure that information/strategies are shared.

8 Be humble

We are often going to feel humbled by what we learn from the people we work with. ASD will teach us a lot about the world in which we live and how we operate. There are many situations when we may feel that we are on the 'outside looking in'. Sometimes we have to envy the way people with ASD see things. Sometimes we can applaud their self-management strategies.

How many hats am I wearing?

If we look back at the range of roles already outlined in Chapter 10, certain categories emerge, as listed in Table 12.1.

Table 12.1   How to Categorize your Roles

Administration Support	Health and Safety Support
• Resource maker • Resource finder • Resource organizer • Field trip organizer • Photocopier • Class records compiler • Display coordinator • Writer in home–school books	• Health and safety officer • Risk assessor • Referee of fights • First-aider • Medical oversight • Drugs administrator
Care Needs Support	**Class-Based Support**
• Bottom-wiper • Toilet trainer • Male/female member of staff for public toilets • Table-manners enforcer • Feeder of those who require help • Laundress • Clothes repairer	• Assembly presence • Supply teaching/cover • 1:1 supporter • Small group work support • Lesson planner • Evaluator/observer • Playtime presence **Other Support** • Minibus driver, technician and trouble shooter

Many of the categories have roles that are done occasionally – maybe once/twice a week. If you work with children who have no toileting/feeding needs, those tasks can be subtracted.

By categorizing tasks, you develop a way to organize your working week. For instance:

Are there regular periods when you could be free to do administration support tasks? Assembly times or in paid time before/after school?

Do your colleagues appreciate the range of tasks that you do each week?
Could you divide some tasks between you?

Can working collaboratively free up time for you to fulfil the different roles you have?

Are there specific terms/half-terms for doing specific tasks? (For example, minibus driver during the summer term.)

Is the weight of photocopying heavier at the start of the school year or at a consistent rate throughout the year?

CASE STUDY

Rhiannon worked full-time in her local primary school as a support worker, with three boys with ASD. Another support worker worked, mornings only, in the same class. At the beginning of the school year the teacher and two support workers devised areas of responsibilities to ensure the class ran as smoothly as possible. Rhiannon's strengths were

- in preparing worksheets and other admin tasks
- mounting interactive displays within the classroom

Meryl, her counterpart worker, was

- a qualified first-aider
- trained in doing risk assessments.

Ciaran, the teacher, was

- motivated to find out new ideas and resources and researched things on the Internet.

The three boys in the class did not have additional personal care needs, but they did benefit from having the oversight of an adult at playtimes.

Ciaran, the teacher in charge,

- took responsibility for planning the learning for her class
- was able to delegate the production of classroom resources to Rhiannon.

Once a week Rhiannon used spare time after school to photocopy and format new resources for the class. She used singing practice

(Continued)

(Continued)

to mount displays in the classroom. Meryl took charge of health and safety matters and the lunchtime administration of medication. She also worked with Ciaran and Rhiannon in planning trips and devising risk assessments. Each member of staff had a share in writing in home/school books and built a special relationship with the respective parents.

Ciaran as an experienced teacher led by example and her enthusiasm and acknowledgement of her staff team was infectious. Each team member was able to use times during the week flexibly, according to the changing priorities of the class group. A reciprocal arrangement of cover and recognition of each other's strengths helped the team to cover most eventualities.

REFLECTIVE OASIS

How far removed/close is the case study from/to your situation?

If far:

How could you gain recognition for the strengths and interests you hold?

If close:

Is this replicated throughout your school or just applicable to your current working partnership?

For both:

List the pros and cons for maintaining the current status quo.

Current English government initiatives and reform of the workforce recognize the strategic importance of having a well-motivated, well-resourced/qualified and content group of support workers in school. For effective education and care of children with ASD, this will be paramount.

To be the most effective in the support role, we need to constantly examine the following questions.

What is my workload?

This needs to be kept under review by a senior manager. You will be entitled to annual appraisals/performance management reviews to focus on the nature of the tasks you undertake. Equip yourself with your own SWOT analysis/an honest appraisal of things you do well and aspects you would like to develop. Regular meetings with your working team (formal and informal) will help to keep workload under review. Having a 5-year plan may help you to examine the importance of your work and where that could lead.

What are my commitments?

The majority of support workers will have home/family commitments to balance with their work. List all of the times/places/people who are depending on you. When you have the time, review your commitments creatively to find patterns and opportunities in what you do and how you do it. With small amounts of delegation/external support, things could be arranged to help you in the most vital commitments in your life. Colleagues can stimulate ideas for how to organize your life to make everything possible.

What are the time limitations?

You can only do what you do in the time you have got. Sometimes we need to say 'No' or 'Not now'. By using the TEACCH approach (Treatment and Education of Autistic and Communications handicapped CHildren; Mesibov, et al., 2004) we can have a visual plan. It is satisfying to cross off or rip up the list that you started the day with. List-making can develop into prioritizing. Tasks for which there is not enough time on one day can be carried over to the next. If you say to colleagues that you cannot do a task *at the* moment – this implies that there will be time later. You will be seen as a realist. The person who infers there will be time later will be respected for their ability to prioritize their time.

How to maximize your potential

This final section can best be encapsulated in the thoughts of our colleagues at the Autism Cymru Special School Forum (2005). When asked how their support workers were helped to maximize their potential, their suggestions were as follows.

Encouragement to use self-evaluation/skills audit

- Supervised monthly
- Annual appraisals
- In-service training
- Informal mentoring: LSA follows teacher model of practice

Points to remember

- The eight attributes for effective practice (Peeters and Jordan)
- Categorize tasks to organize the working week
- Be realistic about your limitations
- Maximize your potential

References

Aird, R and Lister, J (1999) Enhancing provision for pupils with autism in a school for pupils with severe learning difficulties, *Good Autism Practice Journal*, April, pp. 17–26

American Psychiatric Association (1994) *Diagnostic and Statistical Manual of mental health, fourth edition (DSM IV)*. Washington DC: American Psychiatric Association

Asperger, H (1944) (translated by Frith, U, ed.) (1991) *Asperger and his syndrome. Autism and Asperger syndrome.* Cambridge: Cambridge University Press

Attfield, E and Morgan, H (in press) *Living with autistic spectrum disorders.* London: Sage

Autism Cymru Special School Forum (2005) Meeting notes 22/04/05. **www.awares. org/edunet**

Autism Cymru Primary School Forum (2005) Meeting notes 01/07/05. **www.awares.org/ edunet**

Ayres, A J (1979) *Sensory integration and the child.* Los Angeles: Western Psychological Services

Balshaw, M H (1999) *Help in the classroom* (2nd edition). London: David Fulton

Bondy, A and Frost, L (1994) *The Picture Exchange Communication System.* New Jersey: Pyramid Educational Consultants

British Institute of Learning Disabilities (2005) *Transition toolkit.* Kidderminster

Brookfield, S D (1995) *Becoming a critically reflective teacher.* San Francisco: Jossey Bass

Campbell, A and Fairburn, G (eds) (2005) *Working with support in the classroom.* London: Paul Chapman.

Coffield, F, Moseley, D, Hall, E and Ecclestone, K (2004) *Should we be using learning styles?* London: Learning and Skills Research Centre

Cook, L L and Stowe, S (2003) Talk given on Nottinghamshire Inclusion Support Service at Distance Education (ASD) weekend. School of Education, University of Birmingham

Department of Education and Science (1970) *Education Act.* London: HMSO

Department of Education and Science (1970) *The Chronically Sick and Disabled Persons Act.* Circular 12/70. London: HMSO

Department for Education Skills (2000) *Working with teaching assistants.* London: HMSO

Department for Education Skills (2002) *Education Act and Section 133 regulations.* **www.teachernet.gov.uk/remodelling** (accessed 02/06/05)

Department for Education and Skills (2003) *Raising standards and tackling the workload: A National Agreement.* **www.remodelling.org/what_na.php**

DfES (2002a) *Autistic Spectrum Disorders. Good Practice Guidance*, Nottingham: DfES

Disability Discrimination Act (1995) **www.disability.gov.uk** (accessed 03/05/05)

Frith, U (1989) *Autism: Explaining the enigma.* Oxford: Blackwell

Grandin, T (1995a) How people with autism think, in Schopler, E and Mesibov, G B (eds) *Learning and cognition in autism.* New York: Plenum Press

Grandin, T (1995b) *Thinking in pictures and other reports from my life with autism.* New York: Vintage

Gray, C (2000) *The new social story book.* (Illustrated edition). Arlington, TX: Future Horizons

Hall, W (2005) Making the most of the teaching assistant for special educational needs, Chapter 3 in Campbell, A and Fairburn, G (eds) (2005) *Working with support in the classroom.* London: Paul Chapman.

Hinder, S (2004) Lecture on Sensory differences in people with ASD. GAP Conference, Harrogate

Jackson, L (2002) *Freaks, geeks and Asperger syndrome. A user guide to adolescence.* London: Jessica Kingsley Chapter 10: Bullying, pp. 135–53.

Jordan, R (1999) *Autistic Spectrum Disorders. An introductory handbook for practitioners.* London: David Fulton

Kanner, L (1943) Autistic disturbances of affective contact, *Nervous Child* 2, pp. 217–50

Kitahara, K (1984) *Daily life therapy. Method of educating autistic children.* Boston: Nimrod Press

Kluth, P (2003) *You're gonna love this kid.* Maryland: Paul H Brookes

Lawson, W (2000) *Life behind glass.* London: Jessica Kingsley

Lawson, W (2005) *Sex, sexuality and the autistic spectrum.* London: Jessica Kingsley.

Mesibov, G, Shea, V and Schopler, E (2004) *The TEACCH approach to autistic spectrum disorders.* New York: Plenum Press

Moseley, J and Sonnet, H (2003) *101 games for social skills.* Cambridge: LDA

National Assembly for Wales (2004) Workforce remodelling. **www.remodellng.org/downloads/14.pdf** (accessed 01/12/05)

Peeters, T and Jordan, R R (1999) What makes a 'good' practitioner in the field of autism? *Good Autism Practice Journal*, April, pp. 85–89.

Picture Exchange Communication System. **www.pecs.org.uk** (accessed 11/04/05)

Plimley, L and Cardwell, A (1991) Special person activities for PSHE curriculum. Birmingham (Unpublished)

Presland, J (1989) *Action record for problem behaviour.* Kidderminster: British Institute of Mental Handicap

Salter, K and Twidle, R (2005) *The learning mentor's source and resource book.* Trowbridge: Lucky Duck and PCP

Shore, S (2004) Learning the skills of self-advocacy and disclosure, *Autism Spectrum Quarterly*, Fall issue

Sinclair, J (2005) Interview for Webautism course. School of Education, University of Birmingham

Slater-Walker, G and C (2004) Talk at the Autism Cymru International Conference, May, Cardiff

Teacher Training Agency (2005) Registered Teacher Programme. **www.tta.gov.uk** (accessed 05/04/05)

The TEACCH approach. **www.teacch.com**

Tyrer, R, Gunn, S, Lee, S, Parker, M, Pittman, M and Townsend, M (2004) *A toolkit for the effective teaching assistant.* London: Sage, Paul Chapman Publishing

UNESCO (1994) World Conference on Special Needs education, The Salamanca Statement. Paris: UNESCO

Vincett, K, Thomas, G and Cremin, H (2005) *Teachers and assistants working together.* Maidenhead: Open University Press

Walker Tileston, D (2000) in Walker Tileston, D (2004) *What every teacher should know about learning memory and the brain.* Thousand Oaks: Corwin

Walker Tileston, D (2004) *What every teacher should know about learning memory and the brain.* Thousand Oaks: Corwin

Waltz, M (2005) Metaphors of autism and autism as a metaphor. **www.inter-disciplinary. net/mso/hid/hid2/hid03s11a.htm**

Whitaker, P (2001) *Challenging behaviour and autism.* London: NAS

Williams, D (1992) *Nobody, nowhere.* New York: Time Books

Williams, D (1996) *Autism, an inside-out approach.* London: Jessica Kingsley

Wing, L (1981) Asperger's syndrome. A clinical account. *Psychological Medicine,* 11, 115–29

Wing, L (1996) *The autistic spectrum.* London: Constable

Wing, L and Gould, J (1978) Systematic recording of behaviours and skills of retarded and psychotic children. *Journal of Autism and Childhood Schizophrenia,* 8, 79–97.

World Health Organization (1993) *Mental disorders: A glossary and guide to their classification in accordance with the 10th revision of the International Classification of Diseases (ICD-10).* Geneva: World Health Organization

Zarkowska, E and Clements, J (1994) *Problem behaviour and people with severe learning difficulties.* London: Chapman and Hall

Glossary

ABC	Antecedents, Behaviour, Consequences
AS	Asperger syndrome
Austism Cymru	Wales' national charity for ASD
BILD	British Institute of Learning Disabilities
DfES	Department for Education and Skills (England)
DSM IV	*Diagnostic and Statistical Manual* (Edition 4)
GAP	*Good Autism Practice* – a journal published by the British Institute of Learning Disabilities (BILD)
HLTA	Higher Level Teaching Assistant
HTLA	Higher Teaching and Learning Assistant
IEP	Individual Education Programme
ICD 10	International Classification of Diseases
INSET	In-service training
IT	information technology
LEA	local education authority
NAS	National Autistic Society
NT	neurotypical

NVQ	National Vocational Qualification
PECS	Picture Exchange Communication System
PPS	Parent Partnership Services
PSHE	personal social and health education
SALT	speech and language therapist
School Fora	developed by Autism Cymru to give teachers working with ASD in primary, secondary and special schools across Wales the opportunity to meet and exchange information
SEN	special educational needs
SENCo	special educational need coordinator
SENDA	The Special Educational Needs and Disability Act (2001)
SLD	severe learning disabilities
SMT	senior management team
Social Stories	a strategy developed by Carol Gray to teach individuals with ASD appropriate social skills
STAR	Setting Trigger, Action, Results
SWOT	Strengths, Weaknesses, Opportunities, Threats
TA	teaching assistant
TEACCH	Treatment and Education of Autistic and related Communication handicapped Children
Triad of impairments	difficulties encountered by individuals with ASD in social understanding, social communication and rigidity of thought noted by Lorna Wing
TTA	Teacher Training Agency
VAK	Visual, Auditory, Kinaesthetic
WAG	Welsh Assembly Government

Index

Added to a page number 't denotes a table.